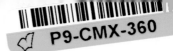

NEW MERMAIDS

General editor: Brian Gibbons
Professor of English Literature, University of Münster

Drawing of an early twentieth-century proscenium stage
by C. Walter Hodges

NEW MERMAIDS

- The Alchemist
- All for Love
- Arden of Faversham
- Arms and the Man
- Bartholmew Fair
- The Beaux' Stratagem
- The Beggar's Opera
- The Changeling
- A Chaste Maid in Cheapside
- The Country Wife
- The Critic
- Doctor Faustus
- The Duchess of Malfi
- The Dutch Courtesan
- Eastward Ho!
- Edward the Second
- Elizabethan and Jacobean Tragedies
- Epicoene, or The Silent Woman
- Every Man In His Humour
- Gammer Gurton's Needle
- An Ideal Husband
- The Importance of Being Earnest
- The Jew of Malta
- The Knight of the Burning Pestle
- Lady Windermere's Fan
- London Assurance
- Love for Love
- Major Barbara
- The Malcontent
- The Man of Mode
- Marriage A-La-Mode
- Mrs Warren's Profession
- A New Way to Pay Old Debts
- The Old Wife's Tale
- The Playboy of the Western World
- The Provoked Wife
- Pygmalion
- The Recruiting Officer
- The Relapse
- The Revenger's Tragedy
- The Rivals
- The Roaring Girl
- The Rover
- Saint Joan
- The School for Scandal
- She Stoops to Conquer
- The Shoemaker's Holiday
- The Spanish Tragedy
- Tamburlaine
- The Tamer Tamed
- Three Late Medieval Morality Plays
  - Mankind
  - Everyman
  - Mundus et Infans
- 'Tis Pity She's a Whore
- The Tragedy of Mariam
- Volpone
- The Way of the World
- The White Devil
- The Witch
- The Witch of Edmonton
- A Woman Killed with Kindness
- A Woman of No Importance
- Women Beware Women

NEW MERMAIDS

OSCAR WILDE

A WOMAN OF NO IMPORTANCE

edited by Ian Small

School of English, University of Birmingham

BLOOMSBURY

LONDON • NEW DELHI • NEW YORK • SYDNEY

Bloomsbury Methuen Drama
An imprint of Bloomsbury Publishing Plc

50 Bedford Square
London
WC1B 3DP
UK

1385 Broadway
New York
NY 10018
USA

www.bloomsbury.com

Bloomsbury is a registered trade mark of Bloomsbury Publishing Plc

First New Mermaid edition published 1983 as part of *Two Society Comedies*, combined with *An Ideal Husband* by Ernest Benn Limited
Second edition 1993
Reprinted by Bloomsbury Methuen Drama 2004, 2006, 2007, 2008, 2014

British Library Cataloguing-in-Publication Data
A catalogue record for this book is available from the British Library.

ISBN: PB: 978-0-7136-7351-7
EPDF: 978-1-4081-4519-7

Library of Congress Cataloging-in-Publication Data
A catalog record for this book is available from the Library of Congress.

CONTENTS

PREFACE

This revised edition of *A Woman of No Importance* supersedes that published in the New Mermaid Drama Series in 1983 in the volume *Two Society Comedies*. Like Russell Jackson's revised New Mermaid edition of *An Ideal Husband*, it has a new introduction to the play, and the section on the play's composition takes account of recent textual research. Apart from the correction of minor errors, the text itself and the footnotes remain unaltered. The collations do not include Herbert Beerbohm Tree's typescripts of the play which Russell Jackson and I identified in the Theatre Collection in the University of Bristol, although their nature and extent are described in the appropriate section of the introduction. This archive provides material for scholars in the future to reconstruct the first performance text of the play. The two revised editions share a biographical note on Wilde by Russell Jackson, and a section on the theatrical and intellectual background to the 'society comedies' written by Russell Jackson and myself.

I am grateful to Merlin Holland, the author's grandson, for permission to quote from unpublished drafts; and to the following institutions for access to materials in their possession: Birmingham Public Library; the British Library; the William Andrews Clark Memorial Library, University of California; the Harry Ransom Humanities Research Center, University of Texas; and the University of Bristol Library.

I have taken the opportunity of a reprint to correct some errors and to add to the list of Further Reading (pages xliv-xlv).

IAN SMALL

ABBREVIATIONS

Reference to *A Woman of No Importance* (abbreviated to *Woman* in the annotation) is to the line numbers of the present edition. Reference to *An Ideal Husband* (abbreviated to *Husband* in the annotation) is to the edition by Russell Jackson in the New Mermaid Series (1993). Reference to *The Importance of Being Earnest* (abbreviated to *Earnest* in the annotation) is to the edition by Russell Jackson in the New Mermaid Series (1980). Reference to *Lady Windermere's Fan* (abbreviated to *LWF* in the annotation) is to the edition by Ian Small in the New Mermaid Series (1980). Reference to *The Picture of Dorian Gray* (abbreviated to *Dorian Gray* or *DG*) is to the edition by Isobel Murray (Oxford, 1974). Reference to other fiction by Wilde is to *The Complete Shorter Fiction of Oscar Wilde* edited by Isobel Murray (Oxford, 1979) (abbreviated to *CSF* in the annotation). Other works by Wilde are referred to by the title of the volume in which they appear in Ross's edition of the *Works* (14 vols, 1908). I have followed the recent practice of giving additional reference to page numbers of the Collins *Complete Works* (1967) (designated *CW*). *The Letters of Oscar Wilde*, ed. R. Hart-Davis (1963), is abbreviated to *Letters*. The drafts and texts of *A Woman of No Importance* are designated as follows:

- BLMS Manuscript draft under the title of *Mrs Arbuthnot*: British Library, MS Add. 37944.
- BLi Typescript with manuscript revisions under the title of *Mrs Arbuthnot*: British Library, MS Add. 37945 (ff.1-91).
- BLii Typescript with manuscript revisions under the title of *Mrs Arbuthnot*: British Library, MS Add. 37945 (ff.92-178).
- C Typescript with manuscript revisions under the title of *Mrs Arbuthnot*: William Andrews Clark Memorial Library: Finzi 2465.
- T Typescript under the title of *Mrs Arbuthnot* with manuscript revisions (not in Wilde's hand): Humanities Research Center, University of Texas. The various typescripts of Act II are designated Ti, Tii and Tiii.
- LC Typescript of *A Woman of No Importance* submitted to the Lord Chamberlain's Office: British Library, MS Add. 53524 (N).
- HBT Typescripts, prompt copies and property lists of *A Woman of No Importance* held at the University of Bristol Theatre Collection.

1st ed. *A Woman of No Importance* by Oscar Wilde (London: John Lane, 1894).

Other abbreviations

OED *Oxford English Dictionary*.

s.d. stage direction(s).

In the notes the names of some characters are abbreviated to initials.

INTRODUCTION

THE AUTHOR

ANDRÉ GIDE DESCRIBES Oscar Wilde as he appeared in 1891, when 'his success was so certain that it seemed that it preceded [him] and that all he needed do was go forward and meet it':

> . . . He was rich; he was tall; he was handsome; laden with good fortune and honours. Some compared him to an Asiatic Bacchus; others to some Roman emperor; others to Apollo himself – and the fact is that he was radiant.[1]

The melodramatic contrast between this triumphant figure and the pathetic convict serving two years' hard labour was drawn by Wilde himself in *De Profundis*, the letter written from prison to his lover, Lord Alfred Douglas. He described his transfer in November 1895 from Wandsworth to Reading Gaol, little care being taken for his privacy:

> From two o'clock till half-past two on that day I had to stand on the centre platform at Clapham Junction in convict dress and handcuffed, for the world to look at. I had been taken out of the Hospital Ward without a moment's notice being given to me. Of all possible objects I was the most grotesque. When people saw me they laughed. Each train as it came up swelled the audience. Nothing could exceed their amusement. That was of course before they knew who I was. As soon as they had been informed, they laughed still more. For half an hour I stood there in the grey November rain surrounded by a jeering mob.[2]

Wilde insisted that his life was as much an artistic endeavour as his works – in *De Profundis* he claimed to have been 'a man who stood in symbolic relations to the art and culture of my age', and in conversation with Gide he remarked that the great drama of his life lay in his having put his talent into his works, and his genius into his

[1] André Gide, 'In Memoriam' from *Oscar Wilde*, translated Bernard Frechtman (New York, 1949): quoted from the extract in Richard Ellmann, ed., *Oscar Wilde: A Collection of Critical Essays* (Englewood Cliffs, N.J., 1969), pp. 25–34. The principal sources for the present account of Wilde's career are H. Montgomery Hyde, *Oscar Wilde* (1975), Richard Ellmann, *Oscar Wilde* (1987) and Rupert Hart-Davis, ed., *The Letters of Oscar Wilde* (revised ed., 1963). Subsequent references to Wilde's *Letters* are to this edition.

[2] Wilde, *Letters*, pp. 490–1. This long letter was written in Reading Gaol in January–March 1897. An abridged version was published by Robert Ross in 1905 as *De Profundis*; the most reliable edition is that contained in *Letters*, pp. 423–511.

life.[3] For an author who returned as often as Wilde to the proposition that art transforms and is the superior of Nature, such claims were more than boasting – they were an affirmation of faith.

Oscar Wilde was born in Dublin on 16 October 1854, second son of Sir William and Lady Wilde. The father was an eminent surgeon, the mother a poetess and fervent Irish nationalist who wrote as 'Speranza'. To medical distinction Sir William joined notoriety as a philanderer.[4] Both parents were enthusiasts for the study of Irish legend, folk-lore and history, an interest reflected in the first two of the names given to their son, Oscar Fingal O'Flahertie Wills Wilde. He was educated at Portora Royal School and Trinity College, Dublin, where he became a protégé of the classicist John Pentland Mahaffy. In 1875 he won a scholarship – a 'Classical Demyship' – to Magdalen College, Oxford, where he subsequently took first-class honours in the final school of *Literae Humaniores* (Greek and Roman literature, history and philosophy). He picked up a reputation for wit, charm and conversational prowess. Most important, he came under the influence of two eminent writers on art and its relation to life, John Ruskin and Walter Pater. Ruskin, the most distinguished contemporary art critic, championed the moral and social dimensions of art, and its ability to influence men's lives for the better. Under Ruskin's supervision, Wilde and a few other undergraduates had begun the construction of a road near Hinksey, as a practical demonstration of the aesthetic dignity of labour and the workmanlike qualities essential to the labours of the artist. From Pater, Wilde learned a conflicting interpretation of art as a means to the cultivation of the individual, an idea which received its most notorious statement in the 'Conclusion' to Pater's book *The Renaissance*. There the fully-developed sensibility is claimed as the expression of a full existence: 'To burn always with this hard, gem-like flame, to maintain this ecstasy, is success in life'.[5] These two theories of the relation between art and life were to dominate Wilde's writing. The arguments of the painter James McNeill Whistler against the conservative critics' insistence on moral significance and pictorial verisimilitude in art also influenced Wilde deeply.[6] The close of his Oxford career was marked by two

[3] Wilde, *Letters*, p. 466; Gide, 'In Memoriam', ed. cit., p. 34.

[4] On Sir William and Lady Wilde, see Terence de Vere White, *Parents of Oscar Wilde* (1967).

[5] Walter Pater, *The Renaissance* (1873; Library ed., 1910), p. 236. This 'Conclusion' was omitted in the second edition (1877) and restored, in a modified form, in the third edition (1888).

[6] Whistler later quarrelled with Wilde, accusing him of plagiarism. Some of their exchanges appeared in Whistler's *The Gentle Art of Making Enemies* (1890) and in *Wilde vs. Whistler* (1906).

triumphs – his first-class degree and the Newdigate Prize for his poem 'Ravenna' – and two failures. Wilde was not given the Chancellor's English Essay Prize for his essay 'The Rise of Historical Criticism' and he was not offered a fellowship at Magdalen.

Moving to London, Wilde set about making himself a name in the capital's fashionable artistic and literary worlds. He had enough poems to make a collected volume, published at his own expense in 1881, and he was seen at the right parties, first nights, and private views. Occasionally he wore the velvet coat and knee-breeches, soft-collared shirt and cravat, that became fixed in the popular imagination as 'aesthetic' dress (and which derived from a fancy-dress ball he had attended when an undergraduate). In December 1881 he embarked on a lecture-tour of the United States organised by the impresario Richard D'Oyly Carte. This was a shrewd back-up to the tour of Gilbert and Sullivan's comic opera *Patience*, but it was also a simple exploitation of the American appetite for being lectured to. Although *Patience*, which satirised the Aesthetic Movement, featured rival poets dressed in a costume closely resembling that adopted by Wilde, the lecturer was taken seriously as a prophet of the 'new renaissance' of art. In his lectures he insisted on comparing the new preoccupation with life-styles with the aspirations of the Italian Renaissance and the Romantic Movement – this was 'a sort of new birth of the spirit of man', like the earlier rebirth 'in its desire for a more gracious and comely way of life, its passion for physical beauty, its exclusive attention to form, its seeking for new subjects for poetry, new forms of art, new intellectual and imaginative enjoyment . . .'[7] The blend of aesthetic theory and enthusiasm for reform of design and colouring in dress and decorative art was derived from a variety of sources, not all successfully synthesized. In addition to Ruskin, Pater and Whistler, Wilde had absorbed the ideas of William Morris and the architect E. W. Godwin. The lectures were exercises in *haute vulgarisation* and not all the sources were acknowledged. Japanese and other oriental art, eighteenth-century furniture, distempered walls in pastel colours, stylised floral motifs – all had made their appearance in English art before Wilde became their advocate. But the influence of his popularising talents was, for all that, considerable. 'In fact,' wrote Max Beerbohm in 1895, looking back on 1880 as though it were a remote historical period, 'Beauty had existed long before 1880. It was Mr Oscar Wilde who managed her *début*'.[8]

As well as establishing him as a popular oracle on matters of art

[7] Wilde, 'The English Renaissance of Art', in Ross's edition of his *Essays and Lectures* (1909), pp. 111f. The text was edited by Ross from four drafts of a lecture first given in New York on 9 January 1882.

[8] Max Beerbohm, *Works* (1922), p. 39.

and taste, Wilde's lecture-tour made him a great deal of badly-needed money – he had no prospect of inheriting a family fortune, and would have to make his own way. On his return the velvet suits were discarded, and his hair, worn long and flowing in his 'Aesthetic' period, was cut short in a style resembling the young Nero. The figure described by Gide was beginning to emerge. After a holiday in Paris, Wilde moved into rooms at 9 Charles Street, Grosvenor Square. He returned briefly to New York for the first performance of his melodrama *Vera; or, the Nihilists* and then prepared for an autumn lecture-tour of the United Kingdom. On 26 November he became engaged to Constance Lloyd, and they married on 29 May 1884. In January 1885 they moved into a house designed by Godwin at 16 Tite Street, Chelsea. Two sons, Cyril and Vyvyan, were born in 1885 and 1886 respectively. In the early years of his marriage Wilde was working hard as a journalist. He contributed reviews to magazines (including the *Pall Mall Gazette* and the *Dramatic Review*) and even for a while undertook the editorship of one, *Woman's World*, which he hoped to turn into 'the recognised organ through which women of culture and position will express their views, and to which they will contribute'.[9] By and by Constance came into a small inheritance, but money was never plentiful. The life of a professional journalist was laborious and demanded a high degree of craftsmanship, but it offered a training from which Wilde, like Shaw, Wells and many others, profited immensely. Wilde became a fastidious and tireless reviser of his own work, and his reviews show him as an acute critic of others'.

In 1891 four of Wilde's books appeared, all consisting of earlier work, some of it in a revised form: *Intentions*, a collection of critical essays; *Lord Arthur Savile's Crime and Other Stories*; *The Picture of Dorian Gray*, considerably altered from the version published in *Lippincott's Magazine* in 1890; and a collection of children's stories, *A House of Pomegranates*. In the same year a verse tragedy written in 1882, *The Duchess of Padua*, was produced in New York by Lawrence Barrett under the title *Guido Ferranti*. Like *Vera* it was poorly received, but Wilde was already turning away from the pseudo-Elizabethan dramatic form that had preoccupied so many nineteenth-century poets and contemplating a newer, more commercially acceptable mode. In the summer of 1891 he began work on the first of a series of successful plays for the fashionable theatres of the West End: *Lady Windermere's Fan* (St James's, 20 February 1892), *A Woman of No Importance* (Haymarket, 19 April 1893), and *An Ideal Husband* (Haymarket, 3 January 1895). The refusal of a performance licence to the exotic biblical tragedy *Salomé* (in 1892)

[9] Wilde, *Letters*, p. 202 (to Mrs Alfred Hunt, August 1887).

proved a temporary setback: acclaim as a dramatic author confirmed Wilde's career in what seemed an irresistible upward curve.

The summer of 1891 was also remarkable for the beginning of an association that was to be the direct cause of his downfall: the poet Lionel Johnson introduced him to 'Bosie', Lord Alfred Douglas, third son of the Marquess of Queensberry. Wilde appears to have been already a practising homosexual, and his marriage was under some strain. The affair with Douglas estranged him further from Constance, and the drain it caused on Wilde's nervous and financial resources was formidable. Douglas was happy to let Wilde spend money on him after his father stopped his allowance; more seriously, he made ceaseless demands on the time set aside for writing. In *De Profundis* Wilde described his attempts to finish *An Ideal Husband* in an apartment in St James's Place:

> I arrived . . . every morning at 11.30, in order to have the opportunity of thinking and writing without the interruptions inseparable from my own household, quiet and peaceful as that household was. But the attempt was vain. At twelve o'clock you drove up, and stayed smoking cigarettes and chattering till 1.30, when I had to take you out to luncheon at the Café Royal or the Berkeley. Luncheon with its *liqueurs* lasted usually till 3.30. For an hour you retired to White's [Club]. At tea-time you appeared again, and stayed until it was time to dress for dinner. You dined with me either at the Savoy or at Tite Street. We did not separate as a rule till after midnight, as supper at Willis's had to wind up the entrancing day.[10]

This was in 1893. A year later Wilde was working on what was to prove his last play, *The Importance of Being Earnest*, the first draft of which had been composed during a family holiday (largely Douglas-free) at Worthing. In October, Constance had returned to London with the children. Wilde and Douglas stayed together in Brighton, first at the Metropole Hotel, then in private lodgings. Douglas developed influenza and Wilde nursed him through it. He in turn suffered an attack of the virus, and Douglas (by Wilde's account) more or less neglected him. The result was what seemed like an irrevocable quarrel, with Douglas living at Wilde's expense in a hotel but hardly bothering to visit him. In hindsight Wilde claimed that this cruelty afforded him a moment of clear understanding:

> Is it necessary for me to state that I saw clearly that it would be a dishonour to myself to continue even an acquaintance with such a one as you had showed [*sic*] yourself to be? That I recognised that ultimate moment had come, and recognised it as being really a great relief? And that I knew that for the future my Art and Life would be freer and better and more beautiful in every possible way? Ill as I was, I felt at ease.[11]

But reconciliation followed.

[10] Wilde, *Letters*, p. 426.
[11] Wilde, *Letters*, p. 438.

On 3 January 1895 *An Ideal Husband* was given its first performance. Meanwhile George Alexander, actor-manager of the St James's Theatre, had turned down the new comedy. It found a taker in Charles Wyndham, who intended to bring it out at the Criterion. Then Alexander found himself at a loss for a play to replace Henry James's *Guy Domville*, which had failed spectacularly. Wyndham agreed to release *The Importance of Being Earnest* on the condition that he had the option on Wilde's next play, and it was put into rehearsal at the St James's. At first Wilde attended rehearsals, but his continual interruptions made Alexander suggest that he might leave the manager and his company to their own resources. He agreed with good grace and left with Douglas for a holiday in Algeria. There they encountered André Gide, who was told by Wilde that he had a premonition of some disaster awaiting him on his return.[12] Although his artistic reputation was beyond question, and he was shortly to have two plays running simultaneously in the West End, Wilde was already worried by the activities of Douglas's father. Queensberry was a violent, irrational man, who hated his son's lover and was capable of hurting both parties. Bosie insisted on flaunting his relationship with Wilde to annoy his father and he was reckless of the effect of this public display of unconventional behaviour. Homosexuality was no less a fact of life in 1895 than it is now: moreover, the artistic and theatrical world accommodated it better than society at large. It had a flourishing and varied subculture and a number of sophisticated apologists. The double life that it entailed was by no means a simple matter of deceit and guilt for Wilde: it suited the cultivation of moral independence and detachment from society that he considered essential to art. None the less, if his affair with Douglas should ever come to be more public, and if the law were to be invoked, Wilde would be ruined. There had been scandals and trials involving homosexuals of the upper classes, which had to a degree closed their ranks to protect their own. But Wilde had made powerful enemies in a country whose leaders, institutions and press seemed devoted to Philistinism and where art itself was always suspect as constituting a threat to the moral fibre of the nation. *Dorian Gray* in particular had aroused violent mistrust, especially in its original form, and a satirical novel by Robert Hichens, *The Green Carnation* (1894), had hinted at a homosexual relationship between two characters obviously based on Wilde and Douglas. Queensberry had made his feelings about

[12] 'I am not claiming that Wilde clearly saw prison rising up before him; but I do assert that the dramatic turn which surprised and astounded London, abruptly turning Wilde from accuser to accused, did not, strictly speaking, cause him any surprises' (Gide, 'In Memoriam', ed. cit., p. 34).

his son's private life well known in Clubland. On the first night of *The Importance of Being Earnest*, which opened on 14 February 1895, he tried to cause a disturbance at the theatre, but was thwarted by the management. The play was a great success – according to one of the actors, 'The audience rose in their seats and cheered and cheered again'.[13] As it settled down to what promised to be a long run, Wilde's career was at its height.

A fortnight later, on 28 February, Queensberry left a card at the Albemarle Club 'For Oscar Wilde posing as a somdomite' [*sic*]. The club porter put the card in an envelope, noting on the back the time and date, and Wilde was given it when he arrived at the club later that evening. The events that followed ruined him within a few months. Urged on by Douglas, but against the advice of most of his friends, Wilde sued Queensberry for criminal libel. The case went against Wilde, who found himself answering charges under the 1885 Criminal Law Amendment Act, which made both private and public homosexual relations between men illegal. Significantly, the accusations against him did not include his affair with Douglas: he was alleged to have committed acts of gross indecency on a number of occasions and to have conspired to procure the committing of such acts. The men involved were 'renters', young, lower-class, male prostitutes, and there was a strong sense in the proceedings that Wilde was being tried for betraying his class's social as well as sexual ethics. Much was made of the alleged immorality of his works, especially *Dorian Gray*. The jury at what was effectively the second trial of Wilde (after the hearings in his charge against Queensberry) failed to agree, and a retrial was ordered. Finally, on 25 May 1895, Wilde was convicted and sentenced to two years' imprisonment with hard labour. In the autumn he was declared bankrupt and all his effects were auctioned, including drafts and manuscripts of published and unpublished works. On 19 May 1897 he was released, and took up residence in France. During his imprisonment he had composed a long, bitter letter to Douglas, later published under the title *De Profundis*. Shortly after his release he completed a narrative poem, *The Ballad of Reading Gaol*. These and a few letters to the press on prison reform apart, Wilde published nothing new after his imprisonment. He did manage to arrange for the publication of *The Importance of Being Earnest* and *An Ideal Husband*, which appeared in 1899. Projects for further plays came to nothing. The affair with Douglas was taken up again and continued sporadically. They led a nomadic life on the continent, Wilde often chronically in debt despite the good

[13] Allen Aynesworth, quoted by Hesketh Pearson, *The Life of Oscar Wilde* (1946), p. 257.

offices of his friends. His allowance from Constance was withdrawn when he resumed living with Bosie. His plays were not yet being revived in England and his published works brought in little by way of royalties.

Wilde died on 30 November 1900 in Paris, from cerebral meningitis which set in after an operation on his ear. The day before he had been received into the Roman Catholic Church. He was buried at Bagneux, but in 1909 his remains were moved to the Père Lachaise cemetery, where they now rest under a monument by Jacob Epstein.

R.J.

THE SOCIETY COMEDIES AND THEIR BACKGROUND

Wilde's society plays, written and performed between 1892 and 1895, are products of a period when authors and critics viewed the state of the London theatre with a degree of optimism – qualified, however, with misgivings as to the direction in which development was to be desired. On one side the advance guard of the New Drama clamoured for social commitment and psychological verisimilitude; on the other, conservative critics, anxious not to lose the newly-regained support of the middle classes, mounted a last ditch defence of sentimental idealism; meanwhile puzzled, earnest craftsmen like Arthur Wing Pinero and Henry Arthur Jones sought out the middle ground in order to occupy it in the name of good sense and moderation.

By the 1890s the distinct genres of the earlier decades of the century had undergone some modification, corresponding both to changes in the social composition of audiences and to the size of the theatres. The values represented in melodrama became more overtly middle-class; from extravaganza, farce and comic opera the musical comedy evolved; pantomime began to accommodate more and more music-hall performers, adapting itself to the display of their talents. Although 'purer' examples of the old-style melodramas, farces and burlesques survived, it was to the new, hybrid forms that aspiring dramatists turned. Of these the 'society play' offered settings in a fashionable *milieu*, literate and witty dialogue and the opportunity to discuss manners and morals. It had the appeal of topicality and a glamour that reflected its audience's tastes. More often than not, it concerned itself with the discrimination between acceptable and unacceptable behaviour, the qualifications for entry into 'society' – particularly those concerned with sexual *mores* – and the requirements of public duty. The sentimentalism of Tom Robertson in the 1860s was supplanted by a smart, ironic perception of the ways of the world, but there was still scope for the impassioned defence of a cherished principle: Pinero or Jones could allow themselves redeeming patches of earnestness. The stylish, well-made French plays from which British dramatists learned (and which they not infrequently copied) provided technical devices and set a high standard of urbane dialogue. References to sexual misdemeanours that provided motivation in French plays usually became less explicit in their British imitations. Adultery was likely to become flirting or – so as to remove all but the slightest suspicion of error – thinking about flirting. Too often it was the machinery of the well-made play – information 'fed' carefully to the audience, surprising revelations which arrive by post, telegram or word of mouth in time for each act to end on a point of suspense – that survived the channel crossing. Grace, wit and sophistication did not travel so easily.[14]

The stage's endorsement of its audience's values took appropriate forms. The *couturière*, tailor and interior decorator often took over from the theatrical costumier and property-maker, and insisted upon receiving their proper credit. Some women's magazines carried reviews of the dresses worn on stage by actresses, as though they constituted a fashion-show. The area formerly occupied by the benches of the pit – cheap seats, occupied by knowing, enthusiastic but not necessarily well-to-do playgoers – now accommodated the *fauteuils* of the stalls, offering drawing-room comfort to those prepared to dress formally and pay their half-guinea. The long, cheap playbill with its bold black type and ink that came off on the hand had been superseded by a small programme, more like an invitation or greeting-card and sometimes perfumed by Rimmel. The air of the auditorium was no longer heavy with the smell of gas – cooler, safer electric lighting had taken over in the mid-1880s and the standards of ventilation and safety had been improved. The producers of Wilde's society plays, George Alexander, Herbert Beerbohm Tree and Lewis Waller, were members of a new breed of actor managers. In the stalls and

[14] For a useful account of the genre, see John Russell Taylor, *The Rise and Fall of the Well-Made Play* (1967). Wilde's borrowings from French dramatists are discussed by E. H. Mikhail, 'The French Influences on Oscar Wilde's Comedies', *Revue de Littérature Comparée*, 42, 2 (1968), 220–33; Charles B. Paul and Robert D. Pepper, 'The Importance of Reading Alfred: Oscar Wilde's Debt to Alfred de Musset', *Bulletin of the New York Public Library*, 75 (1971), 506–42; Katharine Worth, *Oscar Wilde* (1983); and Kerry Powell, *Oscar Wilde and the Theatre of the 1890s* (1990). For further accounts of Wilde's transactions with French thought and literature, see Ruth Temple, *The Critic's Alchemy: A Study of the Introduction of French Symbolism into England* (1953); Christophe Campos, *The View of France from Arnold to Bloomsbury* (1965); Malcolm Bradbury and Ian Fletcher, eds., *Decadence and the 1890s* (1979); Patricia Clements, *Baudelaire and the English Tradition* (1985); and Peter Raby, *Oscar Wilde* (1988).

dress-circles of their theatres, the audience found entertainment and hospitality that comforted and confirmed their own way of life: sophisticated, in good taste, moving and thought-provoking only to a degree that they found acceptable. For this state of affairs the Bancrofts could claim some responsibility. Their management of The Prince of Wales's Theatre (1865–80) and collaboration with Tom Robertson 'rendered a public service by proving that the refined and educated classes were as ready as ever to crowd the playhouses, provided only that the entertainment given there was suited to their sympathies and tastes'.[15]

To the modern reader or spectator the serious plays of this theatre rarely seem adventurous or unconventional. In, for example, Pinero's *The Second Mrs Tanqueray* or Jones's *The Case of Rebellious Susan*, it is the patterns derived from melodrama and the conservatism of the dramatists' conclusions that strike us. Compared with Ibsen and Strindberg – or even with their less penetrating French contemporaries – the British authors now seem timid and reactionary, hinting at problems, vaguely suggesting the possibility of a radical solution but rarely pushing matters to it, and, indeed, sometimes resorting to sleight of hand to avoid controversy. It is odd therefore to find the British 'society play' attacked in its own day as a cynical conspiracy *against* morality, and to discover the work of a rank sentimentalist like Charles Haddon Chambers at the centre of a 'dirty plays' controversy. This dispute and the larger debate about the morality of literature (of which it formed part) illustrate the pressures under which playwrights of Wilde's generation wrote. The terms are relevant to his own fight against reactionary opinion and the immense conservatism of theatrical institutions.

In the autumn of 1894 *The Times* reviewed Haddon Chambers's play *John-a-Dreams*, produced by Herbert Beerbohm Tree at the Haymarket. Its plot concerned a 'reclaimed' woman-with-a-past and the struggle between two friends (one an opium addict) for her hand in marriage. Kate Cloud, the heroine, possessed (said *The Times*) 'something of that *virginité de l'âme* of which the author of *La Dame aux Camélias* [Dumas *fils*] speaks'. Mrs Patrick Campbell managed 'to impart a certain plausibility to this aspect of the character'. She was 'gentle and winning, with the chastened look of suffering nobly borne'. The reviewer reflected that it was 'impossible not to be struck at least with the freedom with which the *femme perdue* and her interests are now discussed on the English

[15] Sir Squire and Lady Bancroft, *The Bancrofts: Recollections of Sixty Years* (1909), p. 83. Although Bancroft modestly ascribes this effect to the dramatist's work, the achievement can be credited to the management as well as to Robertson.

stage'. The play was mildly praised and the tone of the notice was more thoughtful than controversial.

A letter quickly followed from a reader signing himself 'X.Y.Z.' in which Chambers's plot was attacked as representing 'the lowest type of sickly immorality', dealing as it did with 'a partially-reclaimed harlot and an opium-drinking sot'. *John-a-Dreams* was compared with the 'immoralities' of *The Second Mrs Tanqueray* and 'the deadly dull and not always moral vulgarities' of Jones's *The Masqueraders*. A number of replies were published, including Tree's defence of the play he had produced and acted in, and the paper itself contributed a leader on the general principles of the case. This editorial offers a concise statement of the conservative opposition to the New Drama: such plays are not a true reflection of life, as they deal only in exceptional cases; they are merely artificial vehicles for modish didacticism.

> The leading doctrine of the New Woman school, which contains a certain number of effeminate males, is that the thing worth living and working for is the free discussion of unsavoury subjects by men and women . . . The one excuse for dealing in public with themes usually excluded from conversation is to be found in the masterly treatment which lifts the whole subject up to a plane far above that of common life. That excuse cannot be pleaded for even the best of these problem plays. Nor has the best of them that inevitable character which in great tragedy redeems and ennobles the treatment of the most appalling crimes.

The combining of cultural conservatism with anti-feminism (with a sidelong glance at 'effeminate males') and the appeal to a higher stratum of works ('great tragedy') in which the treatment of 'unsavoury' subjects is dignified – these are common characteristics of reactionary comment on the 'New Drama' of the 1890s. The conservative critic Clement Scott argued that plays like *John-a-Dreams* were profoundly unrealistic, in that they treated pathological oddities rather than 'average human nature'. Scott urged Tree to seek his themes in this area rather than consult 'the experience of the specialist in moral diseases'.[16]

In fact this debate about realism and morality in the theatre was only the latest turn of a very long debate about art – particularly literature – its audience and its ideology that had its origins in the reception of the work of the Pre-Raphaelite and Aesthetic movements. The subjects and the leading voices in the debate changed, but the terms within which it was conducted remained virtually unaltered. In the *Contemporary Review* in 1871 Robert Buchanan

[16] Clement Scott, 'The Modern Society Play', *The Theatre*, 4th series, 23 (January 1895), pp. 6–10. The leader in *The Times* appeared on 12 December 1894.

had accused Dante Gabriel Rossetti of a 'morbid deviation from healthy forms of life'. Algernon Swinburne had suffered the same sort of criticism several years earlier, and the arguments that Buchanan had employed – the decadence of new ideas about morality and the decadence of new forms of art which opposed themselves to a socially responsible art – were appropriated virtually wholesale by the critics of Aestheticism a decade later. Walter Pater and Wilde himself were subjected to a range of censure, from the mild reproofs of George Du Maurier's cartoons in *Punch* to violent condemnation by conservative critics in the periodical press. The line of argument picked out the 'unhealthiness' and 'élitism' inherent in certain forms of literature, and isolated a propensity to social and moral corruption – a term which, like 'effeminacy', usually referred to homosexuality – as their most debilitating feature. In the 1890s the treatment of sexuality provided the clearest focus of interest. The controversy about the way in which sexuality and sexual *mores* ought to be represented in art could encompass a *succès de scandale* like Grant Allen's novel *The Woman Who Did* (1895); the hostile reception in England of much French Impressionist painting (and in particular the work of Degas); and works of sociology and psychology like Max Nordau's *Degeneration* (published in Britain in 1895) which branded both as manifestations of the pathologically deviant and so politically subversive currents in contemporary society. Moreover the two most famous casualties of the controversy over 'dirty' or 'subversive' art occurred in the middle of the decade. After the chorus of adverse criticism that followed the publication of *Jude the Obscure* (1895), Thomas Hardy chose to stop writing fiction. Earlier in the same year the controversy claimed its biggest casualty, the career of Wilde himself.

Indeed for several years Wilde had been under attack and had been obliged to defend a number of his works, notably *The Picture of Dorian Gray*. The whole of his critical writings and, indeed, his entire way of life were opposed to the assumptions embedded in such criticism as Clement Scott's. In *The Soul of Man under Socialism*, first published in 1891, Wilde singled out some of the epithets used pejoratively by critics like Scott, arguing that their meaning had been misapplied or perverted: 'unintelligible', 'immoral', 'exotic', 'unhealthy' and 'morbid'. Popular art-criticism suffered from 'the natural inability of a community corrupted by authority to understand or appreciate Individualism'. British journalists had 'nailed their own ears to the keyhole' and sat in unworthy and illegitimate judgment on the affairs of public figures. 'The private lives of men and women should not be told to the public. The public have nothing to do with them at all'.[17] Of course,

[17] *Intentions*, pp. 307–10, 313/*CW*, pp. 1092–4, 1095.

paradoxically no one had made fuller use than Wilde of the attentions of journalism; no one took better advantage of the press's ability to create 'personalities'.[18] This was merely one of the large contradictions that Wilde's career encompassed. In addition, he could proclaim the importance of the artist's work as a transformation of his life and yet at the same time canvass his right to privacy, his essential individualism. In his critical writing Wilde maintained that the critic's reading of a work should be an act of creation in its own right, but at the same time he rebuked the press and public for their inability to reflect anything other than their own inadequacies in judging his work. There were further complexities: Wilde would present himself at one and the same time as both a great teacher and an enemy of authority, unstinting in his advice on art and life but insisting (in the words he gives Lord Goring in *An Ideal Husband*) that the only thing to do with good advice is to pass it on – 'It is never of use to oneself'. The ironic, nonchalant manner, frequent references to 'masks' and 'poses' and continual use of the opposition's vocabulary were a means of keeping the public guessing, of avoiding being fixed, and so 'known'. Jack Worthing, in *The Importance of Being Earnest*, has a hatred of cocksure 'cleverness' as energetic as any expressed by conservatives like Clement Scott:

> I am sick to death of cleverness. Everybody is clever nowadays. You can't go anywhere without meeting clever people. The thing has become an absolute public nuisance. I wish to goodness we had a few fools left. (I, 630)

In a passage drafted for the same play but later transferred in an adapted form to *An Ideal Husband*, Lord Goring's father asks him whether he really understands what he says, and receives the thoughtful reply, 'Yes, father, if I listen attentively' (III, 136). The watchwords of the reactionaries are used with a sincere and earnest wrongness. 'Healthy' and 'morbid' are misapplied in this way: Mrs Marchmont in *An Ideal Husband* complains that her husband, 'painfully unobservant', has never once told her she is morbid. At its best – in *The Importance of Being Earnest* – this technique results in a tightly-controlled play on notions of sincerity and triviality, a heightened awareness of the necessary but arbitrary judgments made continually by those who take themselves seriously and abjure facile 'cleverness'. It is entirely appropriate in this respect that Wilde should have wavered between subtitling his last comedy

[18] For classic accounts of the popular press in late nineteenth-century Britain, see John Gross, *The Rise and Fall of the Man of Letters* (1969) and Raymond Williams, *The Long Revolution* (1961); for a discussion of Wilde's relationship with the power of the press, see Regenia A. Gagnier, *Idylls of the Marketplace: Oscar Wilde and the Victorian Public* (1987) and John Stokes, *In the Nineties* (1989).

'A Serious Comedy for Trivial People' or 'A Trivial Comedy for Serious People'. The interchangeability of terms is, in the world of the play, exhilarating and liberating.[19]

Although Wilde takes his plots seriously, and appears to invest them with some of his own preoccupations and experiences, he takes care to treat at least one of the solemn moments in each play with a degree of irony, extending the principle of paradox to the 'strong' situations required by the *genre* in which he is working. In *Lady Windermere's Fan* Mrs Erlynne renounces her claims as a mother in a passage which modulates from a sincere and moving account of the experience that has changed her intentions ('Only once in my life have I known a mother's feelings. That was last night. They were terrible . . .') to the flippancy of a Wildean dandy:

> I thought I had no heart. I find I have and a heart doesn't suit me, Windermere. Somehow it doesn't go with modern dress. It makes one look old. (*Takes up hand-mirror from table and looks into it*) And it spoils one's career at critical moments. (IV, 239–43)

Presently she is lecturing Lord Windermere on the difference between life and fiction: 'I suppose . . . you would like me to retire into a convent or become a hospital nurse, or something of that kind as people do in silly modern novels.' Repentance, she points out, 'is quite out of date'. In a similar kind of reversal in *A Woman of No Importance*, Mrs Arbuthnot pleads with her son not to pursue his intention of forcing Lord Illingworth to marry her and insists that it is her shameful secret and the consciousness of it which has kept them together:

> Oh, don't you see? don't you understand? It is my dishonour that has made you so dear to me. It is my disgrace that has bound you so closely to me. It is the price I paid for you – the price of body and soul – that makes me love you as I do. Oh, don't ask me to do this horrible thing. Child of my shame, be still the child of my shame! (IV, 255–60)

In *An Ideal Husband*, Sir Robert Chiltern rebukes his wife for having made an idol of him, effectively destroying his career by her insistence on a high-minded rejection of the blackmailer's terms:

> The sin of my youth, that I had thought was buried, rose up in front of me, hideous, horrible, with its hands at my throat. I could have killed it for ever, sent it back into its tomb, destroyed its record, burned the one witness against me. You prevented me. No one but you, you know it.

Now he faces 'public disgrace, ruin, terrible shame', for which

[19] For further discussion of Wilde's attempts to revalue the significance of terms such as 'immoral', 'unhealthy' and 'morbid', see Jonathan Dollimore, 'Different Desires: Subjectivity and Transgression in Wilde and Gide', *Textual Practice*, 1, 1 (1987), 48–67.

(somewhat perversely we may think) he holds her responsible:

> Let women make no more ideals of men! Let them not put them on altars and bow before them or they may ruin other lives as completely as you – you whom I have so wildly loved – have ruined mine! (II, 803–14)

Each of these passages represents a turning-point in its respective play. In each case Wilde makes the moving factor the character's understanding of a point of view that is a complete inversion of the convention: a mother recognises and sets aside the natural feelings of a parent; a mother insists on remaining unmarried because of the intimacy brought about by sin; a man rebukes a woman for setting him on a pedestal. The ancient motif of affinity between kin revealing itself – *la voix du sang* – is evoked and rejected by Mrs Erlynne and Mrs Arbuthnot. The familiar figure of a fallen woman becomes in Chiltern a fallen man. At the same time there is no doubt that the passages are to be taken seriously – Wilde rarely uses lightly words like 'horrible' or 'terrible' – and the outbursts of both Mrs Arbuthnot and Chiltern are meant to be vivid and chilling. Wilde regarded the crisis in Act III of *A Woman of No Importance* as the 'psychological' act, and Goring's references to a 'psychological experiment' in *An Ideal Husband* point to the same interest. To Wilde, 'psychology' seems to denote the investigation of abnormal states of mind by novelists (like Paul Bourget, Emile Zola, J.-K. Huysmans and Dostoevsky) and the investigations into criminality conducted by Lombroso and others. The objective examination of sexuality (for example by Havelock Ellis) also involved 'psychology'. The word has suggestions of scientific analysis, as distinct from moral interpretation, of what would seem aberrations to the 'normal' man or woman. In Chapter IV of *The Picture of Dorian Gray* Lord Henry Wotton reflects on the 'scientific' spirit in which he contemplates Dorian's personality: 'It was clear to him that the experimental method was the only method by which one could arrive at any scientific analysis of the passions; and certainly Dorian Gray was a subject made to his hand, and seemed to promise rich and fruitful results'.[20] This is a more obviously sinister equivalent of Lord Goring's 'psychological experiment' in *An Ideal Husband*. In Wilde himself the 'psychological' approach involves finding the moment at which a reaction or change of behaviour occurs, and in the attempt to produce character subtly differentiated from conventional theatrical 'types'. He may not convince us in the accounts of the mentality of his characters, but we can recognise the implicit argument that their behaviour is true to something other than the 'type' by which the world has hitherto judged such men or women in such situations, or the theatrical convention by which it affirms a

[20] *Dorian Gray*, p. 58/*CW*, p. 56.

moral code. Here the peculiarly elusive nature of the plays is once more in evidence. The rhetoric of the dialogue is sending out one set of signals – orthodox, familiar – but the action is developing in a way that would seem perverse to a conservative critic of the period. The modern reader picks up the conventional element, but the contemporary reviewer of *A Woman of No Importance* finds the play 'Ibsenish'.

R.J. and I.S.

A WOMAN OF NO IMPORTANCE

Wilde wrote most of *A Woman of No Importance* in 1892 while he was staying in a rented house at Cromer in Norfolk; indeed some characters, such as Lady Hunstanton, are named after places in that county. The exact reason for Wilde's self-imposed exile from London is not known, but it may have been to escape the pressures of increasing fame. By the autumn of 1892, Wilde had experimented with four different kinds of drama: *The Duchess of Padua*, a play in blank verse modelled on Renaissance revenge tragedies; *Vera; or, the Nihilists*, a melodramatic treatment of contemporary Russian politics; *Salomé*, an experimental symbolist drama based upon the Biblical story of John the Baptist; and *Lady Windermere's Fan*, a domestic drama exploiting the resources of the developing society play. Only the last of these was at all successful. Indeed, *Vera* had been a flop; *Salomé*, which Wilde considered his most creative work, and which he completed at the end of the previous year, had (in June 1892) been refused a licence by the Lord Chamberlain's Office while it was in rehearsal. Success in the commercial theatre of the 1890s, then, demanded a degree of compromise, both political and artistic. So in 1892, in his self-imposed exile, it is likely that Wilde was contemplating not just an escape from public exposure but also how to avoid the constraints which had been the price of popular success. At this point in his career, with a wife and two young children to support, as well as a lover with extravagant tastes to satisfy, he was understandably keen to repeat the formula which had been responsible for turning the notorious but minor novelist of *The Picture of Dorian Gray* into a figure whom London Society would assiduously court until his arrest and trials in mid-1895. At the same time his own interests – particularly the conjunction of sexuality and power, the most important themes of *Dorian Gray*, *Salomé* and *Vera* – clearly went well beyond the subject-matter generally to be found in West End theatre.

The most striking feature of the Victorian theatre at this time was its faithful reflection and endorsement of social class. Considerations of class both pervaded and integrated every aspect of theatrical production: as the previous section has indicated, they informed the building and furnishing of theatres, audience composition, censorship regulations, box-office receipts, reviews and even the content of particular plays. This was especially true of middle-class influence; it was largely middle-class patronage which financed the growth of West End theatre for which Wilde wrote in the last quarter of the nineteenth century. Theatre building had been funded by the increased disposable income of the middle class. This had a clear corollary: the conspicuous luxury and good taste which characterised the newly rebuilt and refurbished West End theatres were specifically directed at a middle-class clientèle. In general terms, then, Victorian West End theatre can usefully be thought of as a social event; it both defined and was defined by what the Victorians called 'Polite Society' or 'London Society' – that is an élite, upper middle-class and aristocratic interest group. The theatre offered London Society a largely favourable reflection of itself and of its values; and Society responded by incorporating this theatrical experience into its own norms of behaviour – so much so that 'going to the theatre' became by the last quarter of the century an important *social* event, one in which the audience, as much as the actors, were on display.

An important consequence of all this was the way in which the values of London Society informed the representation of moral issues on the commercial stage. In general terms moral debates in Society drama were restricted: rather than question the relative merits of one or more courses of action, they limit themselves to debating how the *given* morals of a particular society are to be enforced. So for the majority of dramatists, and particularly for writers such as Henry Arthur Jones and Arthur Wing Pinero, the main concern was with the fair implementation of this morality: its existence as a guide to right conduct was never questioned. In this sense, Society drama more often than not became one of the external confirmations of the social values that London Society had normalised and naturalised. Given Wilde's intellectual heterodoxy, together with the direction his personal life was taking in the early 1890s, Society drama might appear to be a form offering only limited possibilities. Indeed, *Lady Windermere's Fan* is in many respects a play which observes the moral conventions of the genre. The main character is Mrs Erlynne, a woman-with-a-past, and the plot begins with her attempt to blackmail Lord Windermere, the husband of the daughter she abandoned as a baby. In the opening act the play suggests that such blackmail is only possible given a corrupt and hypocritical society, one for which respectability – which in the play's (and Society's) terms means good parentage–must be preserved at all costs.[21] In other words, Mrs Erlynne's motives might be corrupt, but the corruption of London Society is deeper. However, in the second half of the play, once Mrs Erlynne has been revealed to the audience as Lady Windermere's mother, the dramatic impetus changes. The emphasis on hypocrisy in society is replaced by the tensions of a mother/daughter relationship. By explaining Mrs Erlynne's ambitions and motives in terms of maternal instinct, rather than in terms of a ruthless exploitation of social hypocrisy, Wilde muted the play's original radicalism. So Wilde's first experiment with the conventions of Society drama shows him working with some caution: the radical themes of his earlier work – especially, as I have suggested, the exploration of power and sexuality – can be detected in the play, but they are heavily disguised. More specifically, allusion to such ideas exists only in the witty paradoxes of the play's comic interludes; and the comic characters (particularly Lord Darlington) who articulate those paradoxes have no sustained dramatic function. These are the kinds of limitations which Wilde could have been contemplating in Cromer: his difficulty was to find a way of accommodating the thematic concerns of a play such as *Salomé* within the formal and ideological constraints of Society drama. The rest of his dramatic *oeuvre*, beginning with *A Woman of No Importance* and ending with *The Importance of Being Earnest*, can be seen as an attempt to square this circle.

Superficially, *A Woman of No Importance* and *Lady Windermere's Fan* appear very similar. They both employ the favourite plot-mechanism of a woman-with-a-past; on both occasions that past involves an illegitimate child whose future would be compromised were the facts of its parentage to be revealed. Both plays treat this topic of sexual 'sin' sympathetically but realistically. So, with the revelation of their pasts both women decide to leave the country: Mrs Erlynne with her new husband to the continent, and Mrs Arbuthnot with her son, Gerald, and his future wife, Hester Worsley, to the United States. Here one can most clearly see that *Lady Windermere's Fan* and *A Woman of No Importance* are what the 1890s understood as 'problem plays' – plays, that is, which dealt with the moral and social dimensions of a domestic conflict. In both instances this conflict (as in Ibsen's *Hedda Gabler* or *A Doll's House*) involves the unequal treatment of men and women in matters of sexual morality. A problem which is conventionally defined in terms of individual moral integrity – in this case, seduction, extra-marital sexual relationships and illegitimacy – is recast by

[21] The same theme of good parentage is comically inverted in *The Importance of Being Earnest*: that play is a man's search for a past, rather than a woman's attempt to hide one.

Wilde in social terms in such a way that we see the gross discrepancy of Victorian society's double standard. So in *A Woman of No Importance* both Hester and Mrs Arbuthnot are victims of social hypocrisy, and Hester's appeal to equality in Act II, despite being comically framed in the play, articulates a serious theme. In the same way, Mrs Arbuthnot's banishment both during and at the end of the play, and Lord Illingworth's continued social celebrity, despite his sexual philandering in the past, illustrate the perverse nature of Victorian society's values. This serious element to the plot is profoundly realistic in that it refuses to offer the victimised woman any redress or even solace. Society remains at the end of the play what it was at the beginning: Mrs Arbuthnot chooses to emigrate to the United States and Lord Illingworth is left to practise his charm, villainy and seduction. However, the comic episodes of the play, and in particular the relationships within Society marriages, tend to subvert this seriousness. So, for example, not only are women shown to be powerful (as with Lady Caroline's constant shepherding and mollycoddling of Sir John), but it is also hinted that they are possessed of strong sexual interests and appetites. It is quite clear that Mrs Allonby is a match for Lord Illingworth, and there is the running joke (repeated in the other plays) that widowhood turns a woman's hair 'quite gold from grief'. Importantly, however, this freedom for women, and the social critique which makes it possible, exist only as comedy. In all other ways, *A Woman of No Importance*, like *Lady Windermere's Fan* before it, appears to work within the limitations of Society drama: it utilises and exploits many of the plot-situations of the sub-genre, but subtly questions (via its comedy) the moral judgments they are designed to invoke, specifically Society's definition of goodness and badness with regard to sexual conduct.

There are, however, some significant differences between the two plays, and these all have to do with gender. The first important point of departure is that Mrs Arbuthnot's illegitimate child is a son and not a daughter. This change of sex profoundly alters the play's discussion of power relationships. The concern of *Lady Windermere's Fan* is the generalised power of Society – importantly embodied in both patriarchs (such as Lord Windermere) and matriarchs (such as the Duchess of Berwick) – rather than the power of men over women. In *A Woman of No Importance* Wilde's interests become more subtle, for through a series of relationships between men and women, lovers, sons and fathers, mothers and sons, the play examines the more specific issue of the interconnectedness of power, sexuality and gender. The relationship between these three issues has been a central concern in literary studies for the last decade. Moreover the politics of sexuality has had a particular interest for Wilde scholars.[22] In general terms it has permitted critics to see in his work what is often referred to as a 'homo-erotic' subtext: that is, when read as a whole, Wilde's work reveals patterns of repeated interest which link very clearly to his life as a homosexual. So, for example, in a work such as 'The Portrait of Mr W.H.', which openly discusses male-male desire, we find themes, descriptions and tropes which reappear in later works in different genres, written for different purposes, and apparently about heterosexual relationships. This interconnectedness in its turn points to a hidden politics in what otherwise appear to be conventional works, such as the Society comedies. Hence it is tempting to see the plays as possessing a double function. At one level, as I have indicated, they are placed comfortably within the moral framework of Society drama; but at a hidden and more fragmented level, they can be seen as rehearsing the politics of male-male desire – a subtext quite alien to the conventionalities of the genre.

Given all this, the most interesting relationship in *A Woman of No Importance* is that between Lord Illingworth and Gerald Arbuthnot rather than that between Lord Illingworth and Mrs Arbuthnot (the nominal heroine). (In *Lady Windermere's Fan*, by contrast, the important relationships are between men and women.) In the earliest drafts of *A Women of No Importance* there is strong evidence that Wilde was defining their relationship in terms of male-male desire – more specifically, in terms of the male-male desire existing between an older and a younger man – in, for example, the relationship between Lord Henry Wotton and Dorian Gray in *The Picture of Dorian Gray*. In these early drafts, before he knows of his parental bond, Lord Illingworth's attitude towards Gerald is clear:

MRS ALLONBY

How you delight in disciples! What is their charm?

LORD ILLINGWORTH

It is always pleasant to have a slave to whisper in one's ear that, after all, one is immortal. But young Arbuthnot is not a disciple . . . as yet. He is simply one of the most delightful young men I have ever met.

[22] See Richard Ellmann, *Oscar Wilde* (1987); Lee Edelman, 'Homographesis', *The Yale Journal of Criticism: Interpretation in the Humanities*, 3, 1 (1989), 189–207; Jeffrey Meyers, *Homosexuality and Literature 1890–1930* (1987); Eve Kosofsky Sedgwick, *Between Men: English Literature and Male Homosocial Desire* (1986); Ed Cohen, 'Writing Gone Wilde: Homoerotic Desire in the Closet of Representation', *Publications of the Modern Language Association*, 102, 5 (1987), 801–13; Jonathan Dollimore, 'Different Desires: Subjectivity and Transgression in Wilde and Gide', *Textual Practice*, 1, 1 (1987), 48–67; Richard Dellamora, 'Representation and Homophobia in *The Picture of Dorian Gray*', *Victorian Newsletter*, 73 (1988), 28–31, and *Masculine Desire* (1990).

This passage was taken wholesale from *Dorian Gray*, where the exchange is between Lord Henry Wotton, the older sophisticate, and Dorian, the impressionable *ingénu*. It was cancelled in the first drafts of the play (see Appendix I), but it tends to remind us that in Wilde's work a cluster of concepts – discipleship, sexuality, power, intellectual distinction and sinister male authority – become mutually defined. Two further deleted passages reveal that the other characters in the play – especially the women – know the nature and extent of the attraction Gerald has for Illingworth. So in another cancelled passage Mrs Arbuthnot questions Lady Hunstanton about Illingworth's intentions:

MRS ARBUTHNOT

But does Lord Illingworth really mean to make Gerald his secretary? If so, I am sure I have you to thank for it. You are always so kind to us.

LADY HUNSTANTON

Not at all, dear. The truth is I have never even thought of such a thing. It was Lord Illingworth himself who took the greatest fancy to [Gerald], and made him the offer this morning, of his own accord, which is very much better. No-one likes to be asked favours.

That Wilde originally intended the attraction to be a reciprocal one is also clear. When Lord Illingworth, Mrs Arbuthnot and Gerald are discussing the future in Act II (458ff.), Wilde originally gave Gerald a speech in which he confessed: 'I do hope, mother, he won't go back on what he has said. I like him so much. There is no-one I would sooner be with than him.'

All these moments are, as I have indicated, reminiscent of the power exerted by Lord Henry Wotton over the young Dorian Gray. Reviewers of that novel suggested that on occasions it was hinting at a homosexual relationship between Lord Henry and Dorian. As the textual notes to the present edition make clear, *Dorian Gray* is a source for many of the exchanges in *A Woman of No Importance*. However, Wilde borrowed from his novel not merely dialogue, but also the dynamic of the central male-male relationship. Indeed many of Wilde's works describe a sophisticated male world in which older men (Lord Henry Wotton in *Dorian Gray*, Baron Arnheim in *An Ideal Husband* and Lord Illingworth in *A Woman of No Importance*) instruct and educate a younger man (Dorian Gray, the young Sir Robert Chiltern and Gerald Arbuthnot) and in the process become attractive figures of authority. This in turn suggests one of the stereotypes of homosexual relationships, that of the surrogate father. The theme is alluded to once again in *An Ideal Husband*, where Sir Robert Chiltern describes to Lord Goring the seductive power which Baron Arnheim had for him as a young man:

> With that wonderfully fascinating quiet voice of his he expounded to us the most terrible of all philosophies, the philosophy of power, preached to us the most marvellous of all gospels, the gospel of gold . . . I remember so well how, with a strange smile on his pale curved lips, he led me through his wonderful picture gallery, showed me his tapestries, his enamels, his jewels, his carved ivories, made me wonder at the strange loveliness of the luxury in which he lived; and then told me that luxury was nothing but a background, a painted scene in a play, and that power, power over other men, power over the world was the one thing worth having, the one supreme pleasure worth knowing, the one joy one never tired of, and that in our century only the rich possessed it. (II, 93–109)

The situation which Chiltern describes – the powerful influence of the older, sophisticated man over the beautiful young acolyte – and the terms in which he describes it – a sensual exoticism – echo the world of *Dorian Gray*; they also suggest many elements of Wilde's own relationship with the younger Lord Alfred Douglas. Interestingly, when *A Woman of No Importance* was in rehearsal, Wilde stayed at Babbacombe Cliff, in the house of Lady Mount-Temple, a distant relative of his wife, Constance. Here the intimate relationship between his life and his drama was enacted in a mock 'academy'. In February Wilde wrote wittily of the eccentric 'Babbacombe School' he had set up there for himself (as 'headmaster'), Campbell Dodgson (as 'second master') and Lord Alfred Douglas (representing the 'Boys'). The rules of the 'academy' included 'Tea for headmaster and second master, brandy and soda (not to exceed seven) for boys . . . Compulsory reading in bed. Any boy found disobeying this rule will be immediately woken up' (*Letters*, 333–4).

That these ideas continued to fascinate Wilde is to be seen in another fugitive document, the scenario of an unfinished play which he was contemplating early in 1894, some eight months after *A Woman of No Importance* had finished its run at the Haymarket Theatre. At that time he wrote to Douglas that he was thinking of 'writing *The Cardinal of Avignon* at once. If I had peace, I would do it' (*Letters*, 355). Only an outline scenario of that play, in the holograph of Wilde's friend More Adey, survives. But it too indicates an interest in paternity, incest and a sexual competitiveness between a father and his illegitimate son. The plot of the projected play concerns a cardinal, about to be elected pope, who has the guardianship of 'a beautiful young girl'. A handsome young man arrives at the cardinal's court; he and the cardinal's ward immediately fall in love. It transpires that the young man is the cardinal's illegitimate son, and that the cardinal is also in love with his ward, but secretly so. The cardinal at first forbids the marriage between his son and his ward; the girl then kills herself. The final scene of the piece is a confrontation between the cardinal (by this time elected pope) and his son over the corpse of the woman they both loved. Adey's scenario ends with a melodramatic flourish:

> [He] then reveals to him that he is his father, and places before him the hideous crime of patricide. 'You cannot kill your father.' 'Nothing in me responds to your appeal. I have no filial feelings. I shall kill you.' The Pope now goes to the bier and draws back the pall and says: 'I too loved her.'

What is arresting in this sketch is that the dramatic interest is not in the unfortunate and entirely innocent victim, but in the power relationship between the two men, which is troped in three distinct ways: sexual power, parental power and the power afforded to age and seniority. In the sketch these forms of power are played off against each other, so that, for example, parental power and the power of seniority are used to control the power of sexual attraction. The same power dynamic occurs in *A Woman of No Importance*. The sub-plot of the play is the challenge made by Mrs Allonby to Lord Illingworth (at the end of Act I) to kiss Hester Worsley, Gerald Arbuthnot's fiancée. Illingworth does in fact accost and proposition Hester (off-stage at the end of Act III), but Wilde's interest once more is not with the victim of the outrage, but rather with the effect it has on the relationship between Gerald and Illingworth. It is, in other words, principally a dramatic device to explore the nature of a relationship between two men, once again troped in terms of these three kinds of power – the parental, the sexual and the power of age.

A conventional explanation of Illingworth's pursuit of Hester, and one which would have been expected by the audiences of the 1890s, would concern the corruption of youth. So here sexual power could be seen as exploiting youthful innocence. Wilde's use of the formulaic plot-situation of seducer and innocent victim, however, is generally more complicated than this, and tends to resist the moral judgments which such plots were usually designed to invoke. For example, in *Lady Windermere's Fan*, a similar situation occurs. The play opens with Lord Darlington, the experienced and attractive dandy, pursuing the young and innocent Lady Windermere. However, the moral judgments which this situation demands are compromised by, on the one hand, the play's questioning of Lady Windermere's innocence (seen as intransigent, unfeeling and almost un-Christian) and on the other its serious treatment of Lord Darlington's passion. In the course of the play, both characters relinquish their roles of victim and seducer: Lord Darlington takes himself into self-imposed exile, and Lady Windermere's conception of innocence is tempered by knowing experience – she lies to protect her good name. In all this the theme of the seducer is subtly changed; for Wilde the conflict is not between innocence and experience, but between the power of romantic love and social convention.

In *A Women of No Importance* Wilde's concerns are different again. Unlike Lord Darlington, Illingworth's pursuit of Hester is neither serious nor romantic; at the very best, it is a half-hearted game, and at the worst it is a cynical attempt to corrupt Gerald's 'ideal' woman, and thus to destroy the prospect of his marriage. Moreover, compared with other characterisations of the innocent young woman in Society drama, Hester is a shallow parody: she is mocked by most of the other characters, and is a figure of fun by virtue of her nationality. In this sense, her innocence is treated very differently from Lady Windermere's, and so the conventional interpretation of Lord Illingworth's attempted seduction – where Hester would be seen as an innocent victim – is simply not available. Lady Windermere wins our sympathy by tempering her innocence with humility, but Hester remains only a comic caricature. So where in *A Woman of No Importance* do Wilde's sympathies lie? One reading of the play, which picks up what we know about Wilde's changing intentions towards it, suggests that the issue at stake is one of male jealousy and possessiveness: that Illingworth, in compromising Hester, is disposing of a rival for Gerald's attention, a reaction which recalls Lord Henry's scorn when he learns of Dorian Gray's betrothal to the beautiful young actress Sybil Vane.

If we apply this homo-erotic reading to the play as a whole, other curious or discordant elements begin to fall into place. Key scenes in the play are the confrontations in Acts III and IV between Lord Illingworth and Mrs Arbuthnot over the future of Gerald. At one level the play enacts a fairly conventional account of the tension between parents competing for a child's love. However, on both occasions Lord Illingworth acts less like a father and more like a rival. The speeches which Wilde uses to denote true parental kinship – such as Mrs Erlynne's outburst in Act III of *Lady Windermere's Fan*, or Mrs Arbuthnot's in Act III of *A Woman of No Importance* – are melodramatic in style but at the same time intended to be serious in the emotions which they convey; they deploy Biblical tropes, and they emphasise self-sacrifice and the indelible tie of blood. By contrast, Illingworth maintains throughout the play a pose of witty reserve, and he treats his 'defeat' in Act IV with a composed nonchalance. Moreover his claim for Gerald is not articulated in terms of blood-identity, of consanguinity, but rather in terms of economic exchange and possession. Illingworth makes it clear that he cannot legitimise Gerald (which was in fact the law at the time), but he can bestow his property on him:

LORD ILLINGWORTH

According to our ridiculous English laws, I can't legitimise Gerald. But I can leave him my property. Illingworth is entailed, of course, but it is a tedious barrack of a place. He can have Ashby, which is much prettier, Harborough, which has the best shooting in the north of England, and the house in St. James's Square. What more can a gentleman desire in this world? (IV, 355–61)

However, in the play the indicator of 'true' parental feeling is self-denial. Mrs Arbuthnot has unhesitatingly sacrificed her wordly ambitions for the sake of her son:

MRS ARBUTHNOT

[Y]ou thought I didn't care for the pleasant things of life. I tell you I longed for them, but did not dare to touch them, feeling I had no right. You thought I was happier working amongst the poor. That was my mission, you imagined. It was not, but where else was I to go? (IV, 236–41)

This speech provides the context for Lord Illingworth's offer: it makes clear that his is a conditional one. Were Illingworth's feelings for his son as genuine as Mrs Arbuthnot's, he too, quite legally, could sacrifice worldly success and possessions. By law, because he is unmarried and without issue, Illingworth is, as he says, fully entitled to dispose of most of his property to Gerald. But Illingworth makes it abundantly clear that Harborough, Ashby and his other houses are *not* a gift, but an exchange, and Gerald's presence (for at least six months of the year) is the price. Moreover, the fact that Illingworth conceives of his paternal relationship with Gerald *only* in terms of money echoes that exchange – the secretaryship – which he proposed early in the play (and also recalls its implicit sexual nature). In *Dorian Gray* Wilde had discussed homosexual attraction in terms of a quasi-paternal relationship. The earliest drafts of *A Woman of No Importance* suggest that he wished to continue his exploration of this theme. But the constraints of the commercial theatre demanded much more caution. Hence in the play the line between paternal love and male-male desire, and the different responsibilities and obligations these emotions engender, is much more ambiguous, and a naive theatregoer could have found little to object to in Wilde's subject-matter. Nevertheless, in both cases, paternal (or quasi-paternal) feelings provide an acceptable code for alluding to the power relationship of male-male desire, especially as it exists between older and younger men.

Another minor, and seemingly incongruous, element of the play is the discussion of the 'ideal man' by the dowagers in Act II:

LADY STUTFIELD

Do tell me your conception of the Ideal Husband. I think it would be so very, very helpful.

MRS ALLONBY

The Ideal Husband? There couldn't be such a thing. The institution is wrong.

LADY STUTFIELD

The Ideal Man, then, in his relations to *us*. (II, 142–6)

In their conversation, the dowagers emphasise qualities such as physical beauty, idleness and fecklessness, thereby self-consciously overturning Victorian stereotypes of masculinity which value duty, work and protectiveness. It is significant that precisely these qualities are attributed to Dorian Gray and Cecil Graham (in 'The Portrait of Mr W.H.'), and are features of the way in which Wilde describes the object of desire in homosexual relationships. Equally significant is the fact that these qualities are attributed to an ideal *man* rather than to an ideal husband. By divorcing the terms 'man' and 'husband', Wilde is resisting the Victorian convention of defining men by means of a relationship with women. This moment, which occurs in a whole series of witty exchanges about contemporary sexual conduct, thus echoes a central theme in the play, that of coding homosexual concerns in terms of heterosexual orthodoxies.

A further difficulty concerns the characterisation of Mrs Arbuthnot. The title of the play would lead us to believe that she is the heroine, but the play itself treats her as a one-dimensional character. Unlike Mrs Erlynne, whose complex motives dominate *Lady Windermere's Fan*, Mrs Arbuthnot is simply a victim. Moreover the qualities which make her such a paragon of virtue are satirised within the play. Her plan to begin a new life in a New World sounds suspiciously like a scheme of assisted emigration – an entirely conventional and extremely convenient means of dealing with the 'fallen' woman. And indeed exactly this sort of scheme is derided by Lady Hunstanton in Act III:

MRS ARBUTHNOT

I think there are many things women should never forgive.

LADY HUNSTANTON

What sort of things?

MRS ARBUTHNOT

The ruin of another woman's life.

Moves slowly away to back of stage

LADY HUNSTANTON

Ah! those things are very sad, no doubt, but I believe there are admirable homes where people of that kind are looked after and reformed.

(III, 240–6)

Given this exchange, it seems surprising that Wilde should expect an audience to believe in Mrs Arbuthnot's redeeming career amongst the sick and the poor. Even the room she inhabits is that of a 'saint' – somewhat of an overstatement of her entitlement to be considered a 'good woman'. This apparent carelessness, however, needs no further explanation than the obvious one – that Wilde was interested in Mrs Arbuthnot only in terms of the way her role allowed him to explore the power relationship between Illingworth and Gerald.

This kind of reading of *A Woman of No Importance* uncovers what I referred to earlier as a 'homo-erotic' subtext in which men and women of power (and generally middle-aged) compete for the attentions of young men. However it should be re-emphasised that such an interpretation has only been made possible by the recent development of new theoretical paradigms for explaining literary works. For most of Wilde's audience, *A Women of No Importance* operated comfortably within the conventional framework of Society drama; and, as I have suggested, the play still accommodates itself to a 'conventional' reading – hence its popularity with the West End audiences for the past hundred years. However, whether the homo-erotic subtext was a conscious contrivance on Wilde's part, or whether it was the unconscious expression of some deeply felt but sublimated emotions, will remain a matter for conjecture.

THE PLAY, ITS DRAFTS AND GENESIS

The British Library manuscript entitled *Mrs Arbuthnot* (BLMS) is the first full draft of *A Woman of No Importance*. It is predated, however, by a preliminary autograph sketch book which consists of early working notes for the play.[23] The British Library manuscript was originally written in four separate manuscript books each con-

[23] The present edition makes no attempt to collate this manuscript draft. Part of the Prescott Collection, it was sold at Christie's in New York in February 1981. It is described in the sale catalogue thus:

> This manuscript, described in the Kern sale as a first draft, is more accurately a preliminary sketch-book, consisting of plot outlines, passages of dialogue (some brief, others quite extensive), aphorisms and random inspirations: material intended to be incorporated into a subsequent manuscript, probably the first draft. Wilde has crossed out most of the passages as they were worked into his later manuscript at the proper place. The writing is hurried, often abbreviated, and little organization is apparent; sections of dialogue occur at random, marked with the number of the Act to which they belong.
>
> Lists of characters, some with brief characterizations, occur at fols. 1v., 4r., 16v.

taining one of the four acts. At the beginning of each Wilde wrote 'This books belongs to Oscar Wilde, 16 Tite Street, Chelsea'. These inscriptions are strong evidence for Wilde having changed his mind about either the opening or the structure of Act IV, for some time during the course of writing this act (in late 1892), he turned his manuscript book upside down and wrote the eight leaves (ff. 213–20) that formed, after deletions and revisions, the beginning of the act in later drafts. Subsequently BLMS itself underwent three different kinds of corrections, and it seems likely that these correspond to three separate revisions. There are corrections to the original script made in black ink – some probably made, that is, during the course of the composition; corrections made in lead pencil; and corrections (which seem to be Wilde's last revision of this draft) made in red pencil. The larger corrections to each leaf are generally made on the facing verso. Some of the stage directions and Wilde's instructions to his typist(s) at Mrs Marshall's Type-Writing Office in the Strand are also in red pencil. There is a request for a blank page to be left by the typist on ff. 166–7 (III, 133); this blank page survived through two of the early drafts – BLi and C.

BLMS contains much more material than any other draft (the significant deleted material is indicated in the notes to the text), but

---

(men only) and 69r. (women only). Many of their names differ from those subsequently adopted. Most notably, Gerald Arbuthnot, who is listed at fol. 1r., figures in most of the dialogue under the name 'Aleck', the name used in an early draft in the British Library. Hester Worsley here bears the name 'Mabel Farnleigh', a form also present in the later manuscript. The various acts are outlined in several places: at fol. 28r. Wilde has noted of Act II, 'fin de siècle conversation on marriage', at fol. 72v. he has carefully outlined the entrances and exits of the characters in Act I, while he has noted of Act III, at fol. 41v: 'She consents to let her son go – then comes climax . . .' Various twists of the plot are set down as reminders: at fol. 20v. Wilde has scrawled: 'letter must be torn up.'

Many of the play's most memorable epigrams are strewn haphazardly through the manuscript, apparently jotted down as they occurred to the author. Best-known among these are the lines: 'I know your idea of health. The English country gentleman galloping after a fox. The unspeakable in full pursuit of the uneatable,' which are inscribed at fol. 34v. At fol. 24v. Wilde has written, 'Religion is so close to us we cannot see its beauty, so far from us we cannot see its use,' and at fol. 68r. he has noted, '[women are] sphinxes without secrets, men are oracles without wisdom.'

Many important sections of dialogue occur here in a form closely resembling the later published version. For example, Mrs Arbuthnot's eloquent soliloquy on motherhood from Act IV occupies fols. 22 to 24; her explanation of Gerald's clouded parentage in Act II appears at fols. 45 to 52, while the emotional confrontation between Hester, Gerald and his mother is given in great detail on fols. 55 to 57.

(Prescott Collection catalogue, Christie's, New York, 6 February 1981.)

The process of composition described here is similar to the way Wilde wrote many of his other works (the principal exception being *De Profundis*).

the structure of the play, the stage directions, the situations and substantial parts of the dialogue are similar to the first edition. Many of the famous lines of the play, too, are present. Nonetheless there are significant changes. Hester Worsley is Mabel Worsley throughout; Gerald Arbuthnot is Aleck Arbuthnot in Acts I, II and III, but not in Act IV, where he is Gerald (except for one amended speech – f. 273 – which is attributed to Aleck (see below)). Some of the names of the minor characters (particularly the servants) are different, and the part of Lord Alfred is absent from the draft. The names, places and persons used to locate Lord Illingworth's estate and family in Act II (see II, 375, ff.) also differ considerably. (The original form of these and the possible reasons for their alteration are given in the notes to the relevant lines.) Generally the minor characters in BLMS (particularly Lady Stutfield, Lady Hunstanton and Lady Caroline) are less sharply differentiated than in the printed edition. Wilde also used more stock lines and situations. So Lady Stutfield's repetition of 'very' and the familiar Kettle/Kelvil confusion occur much more frequently in BLMS than in the later drafts. The most interesting features of the draft, however, are Wilde's excessive use of paradox, and the occasional lapses by some of the female characters into over-exaggerated, even effete mannerisms of speech.

BLi is the first of the two typescripts entitled *Mrs Arbuthnot* held by the British Library. (They are now bound together: BLi is ff. 1–91.) It contains versions of the four acts taken from what appear to be quite different moments in the play's genesis. Acts I and II (ff. 1–51) are a faithful (and expertly typed) transcription of Wilde's final revisions to BLMS. Acts III and IV, however, are from a much later stage in the play's revisions, and are certainly of a later date than the California manuscript. All the parts are present in the play except that of Lord Alfred; his part as Lord Arthur does exist in the typescript of Acts III and IV, but not in the typescript of Acts I and II. The form of the first edition, however, is added in manuscript to the facing verso of f. 14 in Act I. There are numerous deletions from Acts I and II. These do not affect the structure of the play, but they do make it much less specific in its social reference. The representation of London Society as openly hypocritical in its sexual *mores* becomes less marked. Hester's speeches in Act II are revised so that the contrast between the openness and equality of American society and the social inequality of Britain is lessened. Hester's original speeches in BLMS and BLi point emphatically to the way that the élite of London Society depends upon an economic and moral exploitation of the rest of British society. These speeches are heavily revised in BLi. Although the pressure for revision here might have originally come from Herbert Beerbohm Tree, the manager for whom Wilde was working, the deletions form part of a general pattern of revision that characterises the genesis of Wilde's first two Society plays. Wilde, that is to say, omitted certain passages for the particular requirements of the theatre and reinstated them for the potentially wider audience of the printed edition. The names of the servants and of some of the characters and places mentioned in Act II differ from the first edition.

The California typescript (C) is also early, although it incorporates some revisions and deletions that are not in Acts I or II of BLi, and hence it seems that it was produced at a slightly later date. The names that are assigned to characters remain constant throughout the draft,[24] and for this reason it appears that Acts III and IV are earlier than the comparable acts in BLi. (It is, however, very difficult to piece together the exact relationship between BLMS, BLi and C.) Once more, most of the revisions take the form of the substitution of single words or phrases or the large-scale deletion of exchanges, speeches or parts of speeches. The names of the members of Lord Illingworth's family are those assigned in BLMS, not those in the first printed edition, but Lord Alfred's part (as Lord Arthur) is incorporated into the typescript.

BLii is, like BLi, composed of acts which originate from different times in the play's composition. Acts II and III are marked by a series of further revisions away from the texts of either BLMS, BLi or C and generally, too, these revisions follow the pattern of minor verbal substitutions or deletion of sentences or speeches. The names of most of the characters (including all the minor ones) and the references to places or titles are the same as in the first edition. Acts I and IV seem to be of an earlier date than the two other acts. The names Aleck and Mabel are used consistently in Act I of this draft, and Lord Alfred's part (under the name of Lord Arthur, as in the C typescript) is included. The time of the transcription and revision of Act I of BLii, then, seems to be nearer to that of C than any other draft. It seems likely, however, that Act IV is earlier. Following BLMS, Arbuthnot's name is Gerald, not Aleck. The misattribution of one speech in C to Aleck (noted above) is, though, *not* in the typescript. Generally, moreover, Act IV in BLii follows BLMS very closely; it shares with that draft many speeches which do not occur elsewhere. One speech that Wilde transposed from Act IV of the play to Act I ('the modern education of women . . .' – see IV, 23n.) appears in both Act I of BLi and Act IV of BLii, another indication that BLii is at least part of an early draft.

At this point in the play's genesis, it seems that Wilde passed a typescript copy or copies of his play to Herbert Beerbohm Tree,

[24] There is one exception. See below.

the manager who was to stage and act in the first performance. Tree preserved this copy of the play, together with his own, his company's and Wilde's revisions to them. The Tree typescripts, which include property lists, prompt copies and actors' parts, are held in the Herbert Beerbohm Tree archive in the Theatre Collection at the University of Bristol. Importantly (and unlike the typescripts held at the British Library and the University of California) they are *acting* drafts, incorporating stage directions and business, some of which must have been the result of Tree's suggestions. In terms of the play's genesis, they represent drafts made at approximately the same moment as the typescripts held at the University of Texas.[25] The drafts held at Texas present several problems. There is one copy of Acts I, III and IV but there are three copies of Act II. Two of them are imperfect.[26] All the acts are heavily emended in manuscript, but the authority of the emendations is hard to establish. Nonetheless they represent an important moment in the production of the final text, because they appear to have been a source both for the first printed edition of the play and for the Licensing Copy. The speeches that are blocked out are precisely those omitted for the Lord Chamberlain;[27] in this sense the Licensing Copy is a shortened and deliberately imprecise version of the performed play. One of the typescripts held in the Herbert Beerbohm Tree archive is almost certainly a fair copy of the Licensing Copy made from the Texas typescript. Taken together these drafts show all the characters bearing the names they are given in the first edition, but the typescripts do not possess the same stylistic refinements as that edition.

LC is the first draft to bear the final title of the play. As I have indicated, it is not as full a version of the play as those drafts which immediately precede it. Many of the references to duplicity, scandals or sexual immorality are removed. Lord Illingworth is, except for one clear typing error, called Lord Brancaster throughout. Some of his most outrageous comments are omitted, and the criticism of London Society made either seriously by Hester Worsley or flippantly by other characters is removed. It is clear from the isolated use of the name Brancaster and from the shortness of the draft generally that the LC typescript does not reflect

[25] The Bristol typescripts have proved too numerous to collate for the present edition. For further details of them and for an account of their significance, see Russell Jackson and Ian Small, 'Some New Drafts of a Wilde Play', *English Literature in Transition*, 30, 1 (1987), 7–15.

[26] These are designated Ti, Tii and Tiii in the notes. Ti is the only complete typescript of Act II. Tii and Tiii are in both typescript and manuscript (in various hands) and are incomplete.

[27] In the notes these are designated thus: (del. T; om. LC).

Wilde's final intentions towards the play, nor can it be taken as evidence of the way it was first performed at the Haymarket.

In general the first printed edition reverts to the uncorrected form of the Texas typescript, although there are numerous minor stylistic changes. Many of the lines deleted for the Licensing Copy are restored to the first edition. It is interesting to note, however, that in one important feature Wilde changed the pattern of final revisions which he had adopted with *Lady Windermere's Fan*. There his practice was to make certain speeches more emphatically rhetorical and certainly more melodramatic. In the case of *A Woman of No Importance* the balance between the melodramatic and comic elements was struck early in its genesis, and Wilde persisted with that balance. Nonetheless one feature which characterises Wilde's revisions to his earlier play, the use of heavy punctuation, is repeated in *A Woman of No Importance*.

The play was begun around July or August 1892. In September of that year Wilde wrote to Herbert Beerbohm Tree from Cromer[28] to tell him that the first two acts were complete and typed and the third act nearly finished (*Letters*, p. 320). The play seems to have been put into rehearsal around late March or early April 1893. Apart from these dates, there are no ways of dating the drafts precisely, for unlike *An Ideal Husband* or *The Importance of Being Earnest* none bears a date of receipt at the typists' office.

We now know that there are more extant drafts of *A Woman of No Importance* than of any other of Wilde's social dramas. It is clear from the evidence of the drafts which have survived that some of the revisions made to individual acts have been lost. It also seems certain that Wilde made fewer structural alterations to the play than to the other society comedies. Thus it is possible to reconstruct in outline the genesis of the play and to locate with some precision the moment at which some of the detailed changes to it were made.

There are, however, difficulties in placing the drafts in a precise order of development. The first difficulty concerns the three early drafts, the BL manuscript, the BLi typescript and the C typescript. In BLMS Wilde used the name Aleck for Acts I, II and III and Gerald for Act IV. In a manuscript addition to Act IV of BLMS (f. 273; IV, 51), however, a speech is attributed to Aleck. Acts I and II of BLii, which are transcriptions of BLMS, follow this pattern of names (i.e. Aleck). The fourth act of BLii, which is not a simple

[28] As the previous section has indicated, Norfolk provides the names for many of the characters. The only critic to pay close attention to the composition of the play is Hesketh Pearson; however, his description of the dates of the composition and of its manuscripts in *Beerbohm Tree, His Life and Laughter* (1956), pp. 65–70, is often misleading and occasionally simply inaccurate.

transcript of BLMS, nonetheless follows it in the matter of names. In C Wilde used the name Aleck throughout, including Act IV, except for the speech for Aleck which is added in manuscript to Act IV of BLMS. In Act IV of C this speech, which is incorporated into the typescript, is paradoxically attributed to Gerald. In other words, for Act IV, C reverses almost exactly the pattern of BLMS. This makes it difficult to see an order in the revisions. If the order of revision for Act IV is BLMS to BLii to C, there is no reason for the sudden change of names nor their misattribution. If the order of composition is, however, BLMS to C to BLii there is no plausible reason for the names of the characters to be changed twice unless the following unlikely sequence of events is postulated: Wilde wrote to his typist instructing her to substitute Aleck for Gerald in the misattributed speech; the typist misunderstood the instruction and reversed the names on every occasion on which they occurred. One has to suppose that Wilde then issued clearer instructions which were incorporated into BLii. Implausible as this sort of hypothesis seems, it is the only kind of explanation that accounts for the anomalous use of names in the play's early drafts.

Indeed the changes in the names of the characters and the places alluded to in the play present the most convincing evidence of the order of the play's revisions. During revision, however, it was Wilde's practice to cast aside a sentence or phrase from one draft only to re-incorporate it at a later stage. (This practice became more marked in the later plays: so *The Importance of Being Earnest* uses material cast aside from *An Ideal Husband*.) The situation is further complicated by the fact that some of the drafts are revised in manuscript to the form of the first edition, but clearly at a much later date than the composition of the draft. There are two particularly important sets of names: those of Aleck/Gerald Arbuthnot and Mabel/Hester Worsley; and those of Lord Illingworth's father, family, connexions and property (in the form of the first edition, Mr Harford of Ashby, Lord Ascot, etc.).

The grid overleaf schematises these particular changes:

Draft	Acts			
	I	II	III	IV
BLMS	Aleck Mabel	Aleck Mabel Royston Sir Thomas Har*b*ord	Aleck Mabel	Gerald Mabel George Har*b*ord
C	Aleck Mabel	Aleck Mabel Royston Sir Thomas Har*b*ord	Aleck Mabel	Aleck Mabel George Har*b*ord
Bli	Aleck Mabel	Aleck Mabel Royston Sir Thomas Har*b*ord	Gerald Mabel	Gerald Mabel George Har*f*ord
BLii	Aleck Mabel	Gerald Mabel Ascot Sir Thomas Har*f*ord of Ashby	Gerald Hester	Gerald Mabel Har*b*ord
T and HBT	Gerald Hester	Gerald Hester Ascot Mr Har*f*ord of Ashby	Gerald Hester	Gerald Hester George Har*f*ord
LC	Gerald Hester	Gerald Hester Ascot Mr Har*f*ord of Ashby	Gerald Hester	Gerald Hester George Har*f*ord

It is clear that the sequence of revisions of the play is not simple, nor even necessarily a progression. It is also clear from the evidence of the names (and from general revisions) that some drafts contain acts composed at different times in the play's genesis. (Acts I and II of BLi are earlier than Acts III and IV of BLi, for example; Act IV of BLii is earlier than Acts I, II, and III of that draft.) The general pattern for each act, however, is as follows (the possible draft for Act III, now lost, is marked thus [?]):

Act	*Drafts*				
I	BLMS > BLi > C >		BLii > HBT >	T >	LC
II	BLMS > BLi > C >		BLii > HBT >	Ti/Tii/Tiii >	LC
III	BLMS > [?] > C >		BLi > HBT >	T >	LC
IV	BLMS > C >	HBT > BLii >		T >	LC

In all cases the first printed edition, which the present edition follows, derives not from LC but from T.

A NOTE ON THE TEXT AND ANNOTATION

The text printed in this edition follows that of the first edition published by John Lane in 1894. There is no reason to think that this edition does not represent Wilde's final intentions about his play, although it is clear that the text differs substantially from the copy submitted to the Lord Chamberlain's Office and from the early drafts of the play.

The textual annotation in the present volume notes the significant differences between the drafts, and, in the case of major revisions, traces the progress of those changes. It also notes the differences between the drafts and the first edition.

Critical annotation of the text has generally been restricted to indicating how freely Wilde incorporated material from his other works and to explaining references or nuances of meaning which a contemporary audience would have readily caught.

The punctuation and spelling of words (principally 'to-night', 'sha'nt', 'one's-self' and 'now-a-days') have been changed to accord with modern practice. Five errors of punctuation in the first edition have been silently emended.[1]

[1]The following emendations have been made to the first edition: II, 427: '*suppose?*' for '*suppose,*'; III, 76: '*that is all.*' for '*that is all?*'; III, 101: '*women, aren't there?*' for '*women aren't there?*'; IV, 358: '*Harborough,*' for '*Harborough*'; IV, 396: '*from you?*' for '*from you.*'

FURTHER READING

Bibliography

Ian Fletcher and John Stokes, 'Oscar Wilde', in *Anglo-Irish Literature: A Review of Research*, ed. R.J. Finneran (New York, 1976).
'Stuart Mason' [C.S. Millard], *Bibliography of Oscar Wilde* (London, 1908; reissued 1967).
E.H. Mikhail, *Oscar Wilde: An Annotated Bibliography of Criticism* (London, 1978).
Ian Small, *Oscar Wilde Revalued: An Essay on New Materials and Methods of Research* (Greensboro, NC, 1993).

Biography

Richard Ellmann, *Oscar Wilde* (London, 1987).
H. Montgomery Hyde, *The Trials of Oscar Wilde* (rev. edition, London, 1973).
E.H. Mikhail, *Oscar Wilde: Interviews and Recollections* (London, 2 vols., 1979).
Richard Pine, *Oscar Wilde* (Dublin, 1983).

Collections of Criticism

Karl Beckson, ed., *Oscar Wilde: The Critical Heritage* (London, 1970).
Regenia Gagnier, ed., *Critical Essays on Oscar Wilde* (New York, 1991).
William Tydeman, ed., *Wilde: Comedies: A Casebook* (London, 1982).

Criticism

Karl Beckson, *London in the 1890's: A Cultural History* (New York and London, 1992).
Alan Bird, *The Plays of Oscar Wilde* (London, 1977).
Jonathan Dollimore, 'Different Desires: Subjectivity and Transgression in Wilde and Gide', *Textual Practice,* 1 (1987), 48-67.
Jonathan Dollimore, *Sexual Dissidence* (Oxford, 1991).
Richard Ellmann, 'Romantic Pantomime in OscarWilde', *Partisan Review,* 30 (1963), 342-55.

Ian Gregor, 'Comedy and Oscar Wilde', *Sewanee Review*, 74 (1966), 501–21.

Norbert Kohl, *Oscar Wilde: The Works of a Conformist Rebel* (Cambridge, 1988).

Jerusha McCormack, 'Masks Without Faces: The Personalities of Oscar Wilde', *English Literature in Transition*, 22 (1979), 253–69.

Christopher Nassaar, *Into the Demon Universe: A Literary Exploration of Oscar Wilde* (New Haven, Conn., 1974).

Kerry Powell, *Oscar Wilde and the Theatre of the 1890s* (Cambridge, 1990).

Peter Raby, *Oscar Wilde* (Cambridge, 1988).

Rodney Shewan, *Art and Egotism* (London, 1977).

Katherine Worth, *Oscar Wilde* (London, 1983).

OVERHEARD FRAGMENT OF A DIALOGUE

Lord Illingworth. My dear GORING, I assure you that a well-tied tie is the first serious step in life.

Lord Goring. My dear ILLINGWORTH, five well-made button-holes a day are far more essential. They please women, and women rule society.

"Full of good things!"

Lord Illingworth. I understood you considered women of no importance?

Lord Goring. My dear GEORGE, a man's life revolves on curves of intellect. It is on the hard lines of the emotions that a woman's life progresses. Both revolve in cycles of masterpieces. They hould revolve on bi-cycles; built, if possible, for two. But I am keeping you?

Lord Illingworth. I wish you were. Nowadays it is only the poor who are kept at the expense of the rich.

Lord Goring. Yes. It is perfectly comic, the number of young men going about the world nowadays who adopt perfect profiles as a useful profession.

Lord Illingworth. Surely that must be the next world? How about the Chiltern Thousands?

Lord Goring. Don't GEORGE. Have you seen WINDERMERE lately? Dear WINDERMERE! I should like to be exactly unlike WINDERMERE.

Lord Illingworth. Poor WINDERMERE! He spends his mornings in doing what is possible, and his evenings in saying what is probable. By the way, do you really understand all I say?

Lord Goring. Yes, when I don't listen attentively.

Lord Illingworth. Reach me the matches, like a good boy—thanks. Now—define these cigarettes—as tobacco.

Lord Goring. My dear GEORGE, they are atrocious. And they leave me unsatisfied.

Lord Illingworth. You are a promising disciple of mine. The only use of a disciple is that at the moment of one's triumph he stands behind one's chair and shouts that after all he is immortal.

Lord Goring. You are quite right. It is as well, too, to remember from time to time that nothing that is worth knowing can be learnt.

Lord Illingworth. Certainly, and ugliness is the root of all industry.

Lord Goring. GEORGE, your conversation is delightful, but your views are terribly unsound. You are always saying insincere things.

Lord Illingworth. If one tells the truth, one is sure sooner or later to be found out.

Lord Goring. Perhaps. The sky is like a hard hollow sapphire. It is too late to sleep. I shall go down to Covent Garden and look at the roses. Good-night, GEORGE! I have had such a pleasant evening!

Ada Leverson's parody of Wilde's comedies in Punch, *12 January 1895: Wilde was delighted by the joke, and wrote 'You are more than all criticisms'* (Letters, *pp. 380-81*).

A WOMAN OF NO IMPORTANCE

Oscar Wilde in 1985 (from The Sketch, *9 January 1895)*

A
WOMAN OF NO IMPORTANCE

TO
GLADYS
COUNTESS DE GREY

Dedication Constance Gladys, wife of the Earl of Lonsdale until his death in 1882, and then wife of Lord de Grey, had known Wilde since 1880. See *Letters*, p. 65.

THE PERSONS OF THE PLAY

London: Haymarket Theatre
[19 April 1893]

LORD ILLINGWORTH	*Mr Tree*
SIR JOHN PONTEFRACT	*Mr E. Holman Clark*
LORD ALFRED RUFFORD	*Mr Ernest Lawford*
MR KELVIL, M.P.	*Mr Charles Allan*
THE VEN. ARCHDEACON DAUBENY, D.D.	*Mr Kemble*
GERALD ARBUTHNOT	*Mr Terry*
FARQUHAR (*Butler*)	*Mr Hay*
FRANCIS (*Footman*)	*Mr Montague*
LADY HUNSTANTON	*Miss Rose Leclercq*
LADY CAROLINE PONTEFRACT	*Miss Le Thière*
LADY STUTFIELD	*Miss Blanche Horlock*
MRS ALLONBY	*Mrs Tree*
MISS HESTER WORSLEY	*Miss Julia Neilson*
ALICE (*Maid*)	*Miss Kelly*
MRS ARBUTHNOT	*Mrs Bernard Beere*

Persons of the Play
In a number of cases Wilde used different names in the early drafts. Lord Illingworth was Lord Brancaster in LC (the family name originally given to Lady Bracknell in *Earnest*); in BLMS 'Stanford' appears for 'Pontefract' (changed in BLi, possibly to avoid confusion with the extant earldom of Stamford); Lord Alfred Rufford was originally 'Lord Arthur Marsden'. In some drafts Gerald Arbuthnot was 'Aleck' — a name used by George Alexander and by Robert Ross's brother; Allonby was spelt 'Allenby' in all the drafts; Hester was 'Mabel' in early versions (see 'The Play, Its Drafts and Genesis', above). Hunstanton is part of the pattern of using small towns and villages in Norfolk for names of characters. Wilde was careful to avoid identification with living persons and was especially watchful over titles. In the case of Rufford (a name also referred to in *Husband* I, 259) he may have recalled that the only Rufford in the British Peerage in 1893 was Baron Savile of Rufford (title created in 1888), the illegitimate son of the 8th earl of Scarborough. As well as 'Mabel', Wilde seems to have considered other names before lighting on Hester: a manuscript note on the facing verso of f.93 in BLii reads 'Ruth: some nice New England name – Mary' (see 'Stuart Mason', *A Bibliography of Oscar Wilde* [1908], p. 403).

THE SCENES OF THE PLAY

Act I *The Terrace at Hunstanton Chase.*
Act II *The Drawing-room at Hunstanton Chase.*
Act III *The Hall at Hunstanton Chase.*
Act IV *Sitting-room in Mrs Arbuthnot's House at Wrockley.*

Time
The Present

Place
The Shires

The action of the play takes place within twenty-four hours

The Actors

Herbert Beerbohm *Tree* (1853-1917) Actor-manager of great power and versatility, his most famous rôles included Svengali (1895, in an adaptation of Du Maurier's *Trilby*) and Professor Higgins in the première of Shaw's *Pygmalion* (1914). His performance as Lord Illingworth was compared with his Duke of Guisebury in Jones's *The Dancing Girl*: 'it has the same wickedness, elegance and polish, with just the requisite relief of genuine emotion which for the moment breaks down the cynicism of the experienced man of the world' (*The Times*, 20 April 1893).

Fred *Terry* (1864-1932) Romantic actor, already established as a 'juvenile lead' (although some critics thought him too mature for this rôle). Married Julia Neilson in 1891.

Rose *Leclercq* (1845-1899) She had been on the London stage since 1863, and had played leading roles in melodrama and Shakespearean tragedy: subsequently 'created' the part of Lady Bracknell in *Earnest*.

Maude *Tree* (1863-1937) Noted for her light comedy roles: married Tree in 1882.

Julia *Neilson* (1868-1957) A statuesque, graceful actress whose first success had been as Cynisca in a production of Gilbert's *Pygmalion and Galatea*. As Hester Worsley she seemed to one reviewer to be ill at ease: 'Her performance was accordingly unequal, being at times too pronounced, like the character itself.' (*Sunday Times*, 23 April 1895).

Mrs Bernard *Beere* (1856-1915) Tragédienne, notable for having succeeded in an English version of *Fédora* — a play from Sarah Bernhardt's repertoire — and (in 1890) *La Tosca*. As Mrs Arbuthnot, according to William Archer, she 'looked magnificent in her black robe and Magdalen-red hair' and 'played the perpetual penitent with great force and sincerity'.

First Act

Scene — Lawn in front of the terrace at Hunstanton.

SIR JOHN *and* LADY CAROLINE PONTEFRACT, MISS WORSLEY, *on chairs under large yew tree*

LADY CAROLINE
I believe this is the first English country house you have stayed at, Miss Worsley?

HESTER
Yes, Lady Caroline.

LADY CAROLINE
You have no country houses, I am told, in America?

HESTER
We have not many.

LADY CAROLINE
Have you any country? What we should call country?

HESTER (*Smiling*)
We have the largest country in the world, Lady Caroline. They used to tell us at school that some of our states are as big as France and England put together.

LADY CAROLINE
Ah! you must find it very draughty, I should fancy. (*To* SIR JOHN) John, you should have your muffler. What is the use of my always knitting mufflers for you if you won't wear them?

SIR JOHN
I am quite warm, Caroline, I assure you.

LADY CAROLINE
I think not, John. Well, you couldn't come to a more charming place than this, Miss Worsley, though the house is excessively damp, quite unpardonably damp, and dear Lady Hunstanton is sometimes a little lax about the people she asks down here. (*To* SIR JOHN) Jane mixes too much. Lord Illingworth, of course, is a man of high distinction. It is a

s.d. LC, T (*The terrace at Hunstanton* BLii, etc.).
8 *They used ... school that* LC, T (om. BLii, etc.).
10 *fancy* LC, T (think BLii, etc.).
11–15 *John ... not John* Wilde added these lines in manuscript to BLi.
17 *quite unpardonably damp* (especially the bedrooms LC; om. T).

privilege to meet him. And that member of Parliament, Mr Kettle –

SIR JOHN

Kelvil, my love, Kelvil.

LADY CAROLINE

He must be quite respectable. One has never heard his name before in the whole course of one's life, which speaks volumes for a man, nowadays. But Mrs Allonby is hardly a very suitable person.

HESTER

I dislike Mrs Allonby. I dislike her more than I can say.

LADY CAROLINE

I am not sure, Miss Worsley, that foreigners like yourself should cultivate likes or dislikes about the people they are invited to meet. Mrs Allonby is very well born. She is a niece of Lord Brancaster's. It is said, of course, that she ran away twice before she was married. But you know how unfair people often are. I myself don't believe she ran away more than once.

HESTER

Mr Arbuthnot is very charming.

LADY CAROLINE

Ah, yes! the young man who has a post in a bank. Lady Hunstanton is most kind in asking him here, and Lord Illingworth seems to have taken quite a fancy to him. I am not sure, however, that Jane is right in taking him out of his position. In my young days, Miss Worsley, one never met anyone in society who worked for their living. It was not considered the thing.

21 *meet him* after this BLi and BLMS add: 'He is very much sought after.'

28 *I dislike . . . say* BLii, etc. (del. T; om. LC).

32 *Brancaster's* a familiar name; Brancaster appears in the early drafts of *Earnest* and in *Husband* II, 634–5. Surprisingly, when Wilde changed Illingworth's name to Brancaster in LC, this reference was left uncorrected.

33–4 *unfair people often are* (unjust scandal often is BLi, BLMS).

34–5 *more than once* BLi and BLMS add: 'As for Lady Stutfield, she is quite irreproachable, of course, but she is just a little too romantic for a woman who has been married. Whenever I find a married woman romantic, I always feel there must be something wrong. However she was very devoted to poor Lord Stutfield. I have heard that when he died her hair turned quite gold from grief. But it may have been for another reason.' (BLii and C are similar.) Cf. *Earnest*, I, 319, etc., on the widowed Lady Harbury, whose hair 'has turned quite gold from grief'.

38–9 *and Lord Illingworth . . . to him* T, BLii, C (om. LC, BLi, BLMS).

HESTER
In America those are the people we respect most.

LADY CAROLINE
I have no doubt of it.

HESTER
Mr Arbuthnot has a beautiful nature! He is so simple, so sincere. He has one of the most beautiful natures I have ever come across. It is a privilege to meet *him*.

LADY CAROLINE
It is not customary in England, Miss Worsley, for a young lady to speak with such enthusiasm of any person of the opposite sex. English women conceal their feelings till after they are married. They show them then.

HESTER
Do you, in England, allow no friendship to exist between a young man and a young girl?

Enter LADY HUNSTANTON *followed by* FOOTMAN *with shawls and a cushion*

LADY CAROLINE
We think it very inadvisable. Jane, I was just saying what a pleasant party you have asked us to meet. You have a wonderful power of selection. It is quite a gift.

LADY HUNSTANTON
Dear Caroline, how kind of you! I think we all do fit in very nicely together. And I hope our charming American visitor will carry back pleasant recollections of our English country life. (*To* FOOTMAN) The cushion there, Francis. And my shawl. The Shetland. Get the Shetland.

Exit FOOTMAN *for shawl*

Enter GERALD ARBUTHNOT

GERALD
Lady Hunstanton, I have such good news to tell you. Lord Illingworth has just offered to make me his secretary.

LADY HUNSTANTON
His secretary? That is good news indeed, Gerald. It means a very brilliant future in store for you. Your dear mother will

46–7 *so sincere* (so upright LC; so sincere, so upright BLii, C, BLi, BLMS).
51–2 *English women . . . them then* (del T; om. LC).
61 *Francis* (Mason BLi, C, BLMS).
62 *Shetland* BLi, BLMS add: 'Ah! here is Aleck.'
65 *indeed, Gerald* BLi, BLMS add 'I congratulate you most warmly.'
65–6 *It means . . . for you* (del. T; om. LC).

be delighted. I really must try and induce her to come up here tonight. Do you think she would, Gerald? I know how difficult it is to get her to go anywhere.

GERALD

Oh! I am sure she would, Lady Hunstanton, if she knew Lord Illingworth had made me such an offer.

Enter FOOTMAN *with shawl*

LADY HUNSTANTON

I will write and tell her about it, and ask her to come up and meet him. (*To* FOOTMAN) Just wait, Francis. *Writes letter*

LADY CAROLINE

That is a very wonderful opening for so young a man as you are, Mr Arbuthnot.

GERALD

It is indeed, Lady Caroline. I trust I shall be able to show myself worthy of it.

LADY CAROLINE

I trust so.

GERALD (*To* HESTER)

You have not congratulated me yet, Miss Worsley.

HESTER

Are you very pleased about it?

GERALD

Of course I am. It means everything to me – things that were out of the reach of hope before may be within hope's reach now.

HESTER

Nothing should be out of the reach of hope. Life is a hope.

LADY HUNSTANTON

I fancy, Caroline, that Diplomacy is what Lord Illingworth

74–8 *That is . . . trust so* (del. T; om. LC).
79 You *have not congratulated me yet* T, etc. (Won't you congratulate me? LC).
84 *Life is a hope* BLMS adds here:

LADY C

John, you should have your muffler. This September air is chilly.

SIR J

I am quite warm, Caroline, I assure you.

LADY C

I think not, John.

The exchange is deleted in manuscript in BLi.
85–91 *I fancy . . . too nervous* LC, etc. (om. BLMS).

is aiming at. I heard that he was offered Vienna. But that may not be true.

LADY CAROLINE

I don't think that England should be represented abroad by an unmarried man, Jane. It might lead to complications.

LADY HUNSTANTON

You are too nervous, Caroline. Believe me, you are too nervous. Besides, Lord Illingworth may marry any day. I was in hopes he would have married Lady Kelso. But I believe he said her family was too large. Or was it her feet? I forget which. I regret it very much. She was made to be an ambassador's wife.

LADY CAROLINE

She certainly has a wonderful faculty of remembering people's names, and forgetting their faces.

LADY HUNSTANTON

Well, that is very natural, Caroline, is it not? (*To* FOOTMAN) Tell Henry to wait for an answer. I have written a line to your dear mother, Gerald, to tell her your good news, and to say she really must come to dinner. *Exit* FOOTMAN

GERALD

That is awfully kind of you, Lady Hunstanton. (*To* HESTER) Will you come for a stroll, Miss Worsley?

HESTER

With pleasure. *Exit with* GERALD

LADY HUNSTANTON

I am very much gratified at Gerald Arbuthnot's good fortune. He is quite a *protégé* of mine. And I am particularly pleased that Lord Illingworth should have made the offer of his own accord without my suggesting anything. Nobody likes to be asked favours. I remember poor Charlotte Pagden making herself quite unpopular one season, because she had a French

86 *Vienna* the reference implies high diplomatic circles. Wilde used Vienna again in *Husband*, I, 69.

92 *Kelso* LC, etc. (Glasgow BLii). There was no Kelso in the British peerage in 1893. The Glasgow title was, however, extant. It belonged to David Boyle, earl of Glasgow, the governor of New Zealand. The name is used for Dorian Gray's grandfather.

94–8 *She was . . . is it not?* these lines occur first in T. After them T adds: 'People are so alike nowadays.' Both lines are omitted in LC.

99 *Henry* (Norton LC, T; Francis BLi).

103–4 *Will you . . . with pleasure* BLii, C, BLi, BLMS (I don't know how to thank you enough LC, T).

110–11 *a French governess . . . every one* T, etc. (a poor relation, a French governess or somebody she would insist on recommending to everyone — I forget which LC).

governess she wanted to recommend to every one.

LADY CAROLINE
I saw the governess, Jane. Lady Pagden sent her to me. It was before Eleanor came out. She was far too good-looking to be in any respectable household. I don't wonder Lady Pagden was so anxious to get rid of her.

LADY HUNSTANTON
Ah, that explains it.

LADY CAROLINE
John, the grass is too damp for you. You had better go and put on your overshoes at once.

SIR JOHN
I am quite comfortable, Caroline, I assure you.

LADY CAROLINE
You must allow me to be the best judge of that, John. Pray do as I tell you. SIR JOHN *gets up and goes off*

LADY HUNSTANTON
You spoil him, Caroline, you do indeed!

Enter MRS ALLONBY *and* LADY STUTFIELD

(*To* MRS ALLONBY) Well, dear, I hope you like the park. It is said to be well timbered.

MRS ALLONBY
The trees are wonderful, Lady Hunstanton.

LADY STUTFIELD
Quite, quite wonderful.

MRS ALLONBY
But somehow, I feel sure that if I lived in the country for six months, I should become so unsophisticated that no one would take the slightest notice of me.

112 *Pagden* there were no Pagdens in the British peerage in 1893.
112–3 *It was . . . came out* (del. T; om. LC).
120–1 *Pray do as I tell you* BLii, etc. (SIR J: Very well, dear! LC; om. T).
124 *well timbered* BLi, BLMS add: 'Poor dear Hunstanton was devoted to arboriculture as I believe it is now called.' The joke was poor but topical, for the term was a nineteenth-century coinage.
125 *Lady Hunstanton* BLii, C, BLi, BLMS add here: 'But I think that is rather the drawback of the country. In the country there are so many trees one can't see the temptations.' In BLii the line is revised in manuscript to 'Nature and I are hardly on visiting terms. I am afraid of nature. She has a bad influence.' All the variants are reminiscent of Lord Henry's sentiments in *Dorian Gray*:

> 'My dear boy,' said Lord Henry, smiling, 'anybody can be good in the country. There are no temptations there. That is the reason why people who live out of town are so absolutely uncivilised.' (*DG*, p. 209/*CW*, p. 157.)

LADY HUNSTANTON
I assure you, dear, that the country has not that effect at all. Why, it was from Melthorpe, which is only two miles from here, that Lady Belton eloped with Lord Fethersdale. I remember the occurrence perfectly. Poor Lord Belton died three days afterwards of joy, or gout. I forget which. We had a large party staying here at the time, so we were all very much interested in the whole affair.

MRS ALLONBY
I think to elope is cowardly. It's running away from danger. And danger has become so rare in modern life.

LADY CAROLINE
As far as I can make out, the young women of the present day seem to make it the sole object of their lives to be always playing with fire.

MRS ALLONBY
The one advantage of playing with fire, Lady Caroline, is that one never gets even singed. It is the people who don't know how to play with it who get burned up.

LADY STUTFIELD
Yes; I see that. It is very, very helpful.

LADY HUNSTANTON
I don't know how the world would get on with such a theory as that, dear Mrs Allonby.

LADY STUTFIELD
Ah! The world was made for men and not for women.

MRS ALLONBY
Oh, don't say that, Lady Stutfield. We have a much better time than they have. There are far more things forbidden to us than are forbidden to them.

131 *Melthorpe* LC, etc. (Felthorpe BLi, BLMS) Melthorpe was Wilde's invention; Felthorpe, however, like many of the places referred to in the play, is in Norfolk.
133–4 *Poor Lord . . . forget which* LC, T, BLii, C (om. BLi, BLMS).
133 *Belton* there was in fact a barony of Brownlow of Belton extant in 1893, but the title was simply Baron Brownlow.
134–6 *We had a . . . whole affair* (del. T; om. LC).
138 *modern life* here BLMS adds: 'We all live in the most vulgar security, and everyone is to be trusted.' In BLi this is changed to: 'LADY S: What a very, very interesting view.' This latter form is incorporated into C and BLii; neither form occurs in T or LC.
146–7 *I don't . . . dear Mrs Allonby* see Appendix I.

LADY STUTFIELD

Yes; that is quite, quite true. I had not thought of that.

Enter SIR JOHN *and* MR KELVIL

LADY HUNSTANTON

Well, Mr Kelvil, have you got through your work?

KELVIL

I have finished my writing for the day, Lady Hunstanton. It has been an arduous task. The demands on the time of a public man are very heavy nowadays, very heavy indeed. And I don't think they meet with adequate recognition.

LADY CAROLINE

John, have you got your overshoes on?

SIR JOHN

Yes, my love.

LADY CAROLINE

I think you had better come over here, John. It is more sheltered.

SIR JOHN

I am quite comfortable, Caroline.

LADY CAROLINE

I think not, John. You had better sit beside me.

SIR JOHN *rises and goes across*

LADY STUTFIELD

And what have you been writing about this morning, Mr Kelvil?

KELVIL

On the usual subject, Lady Stutfield. On Purity.

LADY STUTFIELD

That must be such a very, very interesting thing to write about.

152 *thought of that* T has a further exchange:

LADY C

Your last remark, Mrs Allenby, seems to me to sound rather like tempting Providence.

MRS AL

Oh! surely Providence can resist temptation by this time, Lady Caroline.

These lines were eventually used in *Husband*, III, 378–9.

160 *I think you* before this sentence BLi and BLMS have: 'You should have brought a muffler, too. What is the use of my always knitting mufflers for you if you don't wear them.' The lines are deleted in manuscript in BLi and moved to I, 11–13.

163 *You had ... me* BLii, etc. (om. LC, T).

164–5 *And what ... Mr Kelvil* LC, T, (om. BLii, C, BLi, BLMS).

166 *Purity* see Introduction.

KELVIL

It is the one subject of really national importance, nowadays, Lady Stutfield. I purpose addressing my constituents on the question before Parliament meets. I find that the poorer classes of this country display a marked desire for a higher ethical standard.

LADY STUTFIELD

How quite, quite nice of them.

LADY CAROLINE

Are you in favour of women taking part in politics, Mr Kettle?

SIR JOHN

Kelvil, my love, Kelvil.

KELVIL

The growing influence of women is the one reassuring thing in our political life, Lady Caroline. Women are always on the side of morality, public and private.

LADY STUTFIELD

It is so very, very gratifying to hear you say that.

LADY HUNSTANTON

Ah, yes! the moral qualities in women – that is the important thing. I am afraid, Caroline, that dear Lord Illingworth doesn't value the moral qualities in women as much as he should.

Enter LORD ILLINGWORTH

LADY STUTFIELD

The world says that Lord Illingworth is very, very wicked.

173 *ethical standard* T adds 'among the upper classes' and so repeats a familiar joke. Cf. *Earnest* II, 249–50, where Dr Chasuble lectures on behalf of 'the Society for the Prevention of Discontent among the Upper Orders' and note to *Husband*, II, 510.

175–7 *Are you . . . my love, Kelvil* T, etc. (om. LC). In T the preceding speech is given to Mrs Allenby, not Lady C.

184–5 *as he should* after Lady H's speech, T, BLii, C, BLi, BLMS have a speech for Lord I as he enters:

> LORD I
>
> How can you say that, Lady Hunstanton? Of course I think it is better to be beautiful than to be good. But on the other hand, no one is more ready to admit that it is better to be good than to be ugly.
>
> The deleted line was taken from *Dorian Gray* (*DG*, pp. 194–5/*CW*, p. 147.)

186–92 *The world says . . . entirely true* a familiar paradox. Cf. *LWF* I, 148–151 and *Dorian Gray:*

> 'Everybody I know says you are very wicked,' cried the old lady shaking her head.
>
> Lord Henry looked serious for some moments. 'It is perfectly monstrous,' he said at last, 'the way people go about nowadays saying things against one behind one's back that are absolutely and entirely true.' (*DG*, pp. 178–9/ *CW*, p. 136.)

LORD ILLINGWORTH
But what world says that, Lady Stutfield? It must be the next world. This world and I are on excellent terms.
Sits down beside MRS ALLONBY

LADY STUTFIELD
Everyone *I* know says you are very, very wicked.

LORD ILLINGWORTH
It is perfectly monstrous the way people go about, nowadays, saying things against one behind one's back that are absolutely and entirely true.

LADY HUNSTANTON
Dear Lord Illingworth is quite hopeless, Lady Stutfield. I have given up trying to reform him. It would take a Public Company with a Board of Directors and a paid Secretary to do that. But you have the secretary already, Lord Illingworth, haven't you? Gerald Arbuthnot has told us of his good fortune; it is really most kind of you.

LORD ILLINGWORTH
Oh, don't say that, Lady Hunstanton. Kind is a dreadful word. I took a great fancy to young Arbuthnot the moment I met him, and he'll be of considerable use to me in something I am foolish enough to think of doing.

LADY HUNSTANTON
He is an admirable young man. And his mother is one of my dearest friends. He has just gone for a walk with our pretty American. She is very pretty, is she not?

LADY CAROLINE
Far too pretty. These American girls carry off all the good

194–5 *Public Company* ... *paid Secretary* the term suggests a specifically topical reference, but in fact the most recent Act controlling public companies was the 1845 Companies Clauses Consolidation Act. (It was however amended in 1888 and 1889 and there was other company law legislation in 1891 and 1892.)

201–2 *and he'll* ... *of doing* C (He is quite charming in every way! And he will be excessively useful to me. I never answer my letters, and as I get a perfectly unbearable amount every morning, I want someone to help me not to answer them. BLi, BLMS).

203 *He is an* before this sentence BLMS adds: 'Well, you'll find him most willing and pleasant.' (The line is deleted in BLi.)

206 *These American girls carry off* LC, etc. (These American girls are a great source of trouble to mothers who have marriageable daughters. They carry off BLMS). A familiar joke, repeated by Hester in II, 250. Cf. Virginia Otis's marriage to the Duke of Cheshire in 'The Canterville Ghost': 'For Virginia received the coronet which is the reward of all good little American girls.' (*CSF*, p. 86/*CW*, p. 213.) Cf. also *Dorian Gray*: 'Why can't these American women stay in their own country?'

matches. Why can't they stay in their own country? They are always telling us it is the Paradise of women.

LORD ILLINGWORTH
It is, Lady Caroline. That is why, like Eve, they are so extremely anxious to get out of it.

LADY CAROLINE
Who are Miss Worsley's parents?

LORD ILLINGWORTH
American women are wonderfully clever in concealing their parents.

LADY HUNSTANTON
My dear Lord Illingworth, what do you mean? Miss Worsley, Caroline, is an orphan. Her father was a very wealthy millionaire, or philanthropist, or both, I believe, who entertained my son quite hospitably, when he visited Boston. I don't know how he made his money, originally.

KELVIL
I fancy in American dry goods.

LADY HUNSTANTON
What are American dry goods?

LORD ILLINGWORTH
American novels.

LADY HUNSTANTON
How very singular! . . . Well, from whatever source her large

They are always telling us it is the Paradise for women'. (*DG*, p. 34/*CW*, p. 40.) Most of the material on Americans recalls Wilde's article 'The American Invasion', published in 1887 (in *The Court and Society Review;* see *Miscellanies,* pp. 77-82).

212–3 *American women . . . their parents* LC, T (That is a question no one can answer about any American. American women are as clever in concealing their parents as English women are in concealing their pasts C, BLii). The reworking of this line emphasises a feature common to many of Wilde's revisions — the stressing of the insularity of London Society and a less explicitly critical representation of its sexual *mores*.

219 *dry goods* BLi and BLMS add after this line: 'I think I remember the name in connection with a question of Tariff duties.'

220–1 *What are . . . American novels* another quotation from *Dorian Gray*:

'Dry goods! What are American dry-goods?' asked the Duchess, raising her large hands in wonder and accentuating the verb. 'American novels,' answered Lord Henry. (*DG*, p. 38/*CW*, p. 42.)

American novels were a favourite butt for Wilde. Cf. 'Lord Arthur Savile's Crime':

'I don't think I like American inventions, Arthur. I am quite sure I don't. I read some American novels lately, and they were quite nonsensical.' (*CSF*, p. 36/*CW*, p. 181.)

fortune came, I have a great esteem for Miss Worsley. She dresses exceedingly well. All Americans do dress well. They get their clothes in Paris.

MRS ALLONBY

They say, Lady Hunstanton, that when good Americans die they go to Paris.

LADY HUNSTANTON

Indeed? And when bad Americans die, where do they go to?

LORD ILLINGWORTH

Oh, they go to America.

KELVIL

I am afraid you don't appreciate America, Lord Illingworth. It is a very remarkable country, especially considering its youth.

LORD ILLINGWORTH

The youth of America is their oldest tradition. It has been going on now for three hundred years. To hear them talk one would imagine they were in their first childhood. As far as civilisation goes they are in their second.

KELVIL

There is undoubtedly a great deal of corruption in American politics. I suppose you allude to that?

223–4 *She dresses exceedingly well* LC, etc. (She is a little formal in her views, but she dresses exceedingly well C, BLi, BLMS). The original line highlights one of the play's central themes, the opposition between style and morality.

224–30 *All Americans . . . to America* another quotation from *Dorian Gray*:
'And they dress well, too. They get all their dresses in Paris. I wish I could afford to do the same.'
'They say that when good Americans die they go to Paris,' chuckled Sir Thomas [. . .]
'Really! And where do bad Americans go when they die?' inquired the Duchess.
'They go to America,' murmured Lord Henry. (*DG*, p. 38/*CW*, p. 43.)

228–9 *And when . . . go to?* in BLMS Lady H's question is addressed to Mr Kettle and Sir J's familiar correction follows. The deletion of this line in BLi indicates that Wilde himself suspected that the opening of the play contained too many stereotyped comic situations.

237 *in their second* BLii, C, BLi, BLMS add: 'They are worn out without ever having been wicked, which is a mistake, and corrupt without ever having been cultured, which is a crime.'

238–9 *corruption in American politics* a fairly widespread opinion. Cf. W.E. Adams, *Our American Cousins* (1883), pp. 116–7: 'American politics, almost everywhere outside America, are believed to be corrupt — in fact, rotten to the core [. . .] Even in America itself the evil is openly discussed.'

LORD ILLINGWORTH
I wonder.

LADY HUNSTANTON
Politics are in a very sad way everywhere, I am told. They certainly are in England. Dear Mr Cardew is ruining the country. I wonder Mrs Cardew allows him. I am sure, Lord Illingworth, you don't think that uneducated people should be allowed to have votes?

LORD ILLINGWORTH
I think they are the only people who should.

KELVIL
Do you take no side then in modern politics, Lord Illingworth?

LORD ILLINGWORTH
One should never take sides in anything, Mr Kelvil. Taking sides is the beginning of sincerity, and earnestness follows shortly afterwards, and the human being becomes a bore. However, the House of Commons really does very little harm. You can't make people good by Act of Parliament, – that is something.

KELVIL
You cannot deny that the House of Commons has always shown great sympathy with the sufferings of the poor.

LORD ILLINGWORTH
That is its special vice. That is the special vice of the age. One should sympathise with the joy, the beauty, the colour of life. The less said about life's sores the better, Mr Kelvil.

KELVIL
Still our East End is a very important problem.

LORD ILLINGWORTH
Quite so. It is the problem of slavery. And we are trying to solve it by amusing the slaves.

246 *people who should* see Appendix I.
257–62 *One should sympathise ... amusing the slaves* another direct quotation from *Dorian Gray*:
'One should sympathise with the colour, the beauty, the joy of life. The less said about life's sores the better.'
'Still, the East End is a very important problem,' remarked Sir Thomas, with a grave shake of the head. 'Quite so,' answered the young Lord. 'It is the problem of slavery, and we try to solve it by amusing the slaves.' (*DG* p. 40/*CW*, p. 44.) Cf. also 'The Soul of Man Under Socialism': 'One should sympathise with the entirety of life, not with life's sores and maladies merely, but with life's joy and beauty and energy and health and freedom.' (*Intentions*, p. 329/*CW*, p. 1101.)

LADY HUNSTANTON

Certainly, a great deal may be done by means of cheap entertainments, as you say, Lord Illingworth. Dear Dr Daubeny, our rector here, provides, with the assistance of his curates, really admirable recreations for the poor during the winter. And much good may be done by means of a magic lantern, or a missionary, or some popular amusement of that kind.

LADY CAROLINE

I am not at all in favour of amusements for the poor, Jane. Blankets and coals are sufficient. There is too much love of pleasure amongst the upper classes as it is. Health is what we want in modern life. The tone is not healthy, not healthy at all.

KELVIL

You are quite right, Lady Caroline.

LADY CAROLINE

I believe I am usually right.

MRS ALLONBY

Horrid word 'health.'

LORD ILLINGWORTH

Silliest word in our language, and one knows so well the popular idea of health. The English country gentleman galloping after a fox – the unspeakable in full pursuit of the uneatable.

KELVIL

May I ask, Lord Illingworth, if you regard the House of Lords as a better institution than the House of Commons?

267–9 *magic lantern . . . that kind* LC, T (magic lantern that has been nearly eaten by savages, or a missionary with slides . . . I mean, you know what I mean BLii, C, BLi, BLMS).

271 *Blankets and coals* the traditional gifts of the gentry for their less fortunate and less wealthy neighbours.

275–6 *You are quite . . . usually right* (om. BLii, C, BLi, BLMS:

KELVIL: You are quite right, Lady Caroline.

LADY CAROLINE:

I believe I am usually right, Mr Kettle.

SIR JOHN

Kelvil, my own one, Kelvil. LC, T).

277 *Horrid word 'health'* a topic popular with Wilde, connoting moral as well as physical health. Cf. 'The Soul of Man Under Socialism', where Wilde tried to redefine 'healthy' and 'unhealthy' art: 'the popular novel that the public call healthy is always a thoroughly unhealthy production; and what the public call an unhealthy novel is always a beautiful and healthy work of art.' (*Intentions* p. 310/*CW*, p. 1094.)

278 *Silliest word in our language* BLii, etc. (del. T; om. LC).

LORD ILLINGWORTH
A much better institution, of course. We in the House of Lords are never in touch with public opinion. That makes us a civilised body.

KELVIL
Are you serious in putting forward such a view?

LORD ILLINGWORTH
Quite serious, Mr Kelvil. (*To* MRS ALLONBY) Vulgar habit that is people have nowadays of asking one, after one has given them an idea, whether one is serious or not. Nothing is serious except passion. The intellect is not a serious thing, and never has been. It is an instrument on which one plays, that is all. The only serious form of intellect I know is the British intellect. And on the British intellect the illiterates play the drum.

LADY HUNSTANTON
What are you saying, Lord Illingworth, about the drum?

LORD ILLINGWORTH
I was merely talking to Mrs Allonby about the leading articles in the London newspapers.

LADY HUNSTANTON
But do you believe all that is written in the newspapers?

LORD ILLINGWORTH
I do. Nowadays it is only the unreadable that occurs.
Rises with MRS ALLONBY

LADY HUNSTANTON
Are you going, Mrs Allonby?

MRS ALLONBY
Just as far as the conservatory. Lord Illingworth told me this morning that there was an orchid there as beautiful as the seven deadly sins.

LADY HUNSTANTON
My dear, I hope there is nothing of the kind. I will certainly

284–6 *A much . . . civilised body* LC, T (All institutions are wrong. But at least we in the House of Lords are never in touch with public opinion. That makes us a civilised body.
KELVIL
The opinion of the many is what is always to be followed.
LORD I
Majorities are always wrong, and minorities are never right. BLii, C, BLi, BLMS).

293–300 *The only serious . . . that occurs* T, etc. (om. LC).

speak to the gardener.

Exit MRS ALLONBY *and* LORD ILLINGWORTH

LADY CAROLINE
Remarkable type, Mrs Allonby.

LADY HUNSTANTON
She lets her clever tongue run away with her sometimes.

LADY CAROLINE
Is that the only thing, Jane, Mrs Allonby allows to run away with her?

LADY HUNSTANTON
I hope so, Caroline, I am sure.

Enter LORD ALFRED

Dear Lord Alfred, do join us.

LORD ALFRED *sits down beside* LADY STUTFIELD

LADY CAROLINE
You believe good of every one, Jane. It is a great fault.

LADY STUTFIELD
Do you really, really think, Lady Caroline, that one should believe evil of every one?

LADY CAROLINE
I think it is much safer to do so, Lady Stutfield. Until, of course, people are found out to be good. But that requires a great deal of investigation, nowadays.

LADY STUTFIELD
But there is so much unkind scandal in modern life.

LADY CAROLINE
Lord Illingworth remarked to me last night at dinner that the basis of every scandal is an absolutely immoral certainty.

KELVIL
Lord Illingworth is, of course, a very brilliant man, but he seems to me to be lacking in that fine faith in the nobility and purity of life which is so important in this century.

312 s.d. Lord Alfred is not in BLMS. His part, as Lord Arthur, is a manuscript addition to BLi which is subsequently incorporated into BLii, C and successive drafts.

314–21 *Do you really . . . absolutely immoral certainty* BLii, etc. (del. T; om. LC). After the last speech by Lady C, BLi and BLMS add: 'It is an excellent phrase.' The play on the idea of moral certainty is taken virtually verbatim from *Dorian Gray:* 'You are talking scandal, Henry, and there is never any basis for scandal.'

'The basis for every scandal is an immoral certainty,' said Lord Henry, lighting a cigarette. (*DG*, p. 204/*CW*, p. 154.)

LADY STUTFIELD
Yes, quite, quite important, is it not?

KELVIL
He gives me the impression of a man who does not appreciate the beauty of our English home-life. I would say that he was tainted with foreign ideas on the subject.

LADY STUTFIELD
There is nothing, nothing like the beauty of home-life, is there?

KELVIL
It is the mainstay of our moral system in England, Lady Stutfield. Without it we would become like our neighbours.

LADY STUTFIELD
That would be so, so sad, would it not?

KELVIL
I am afraid, too, that Lord Illingworth regards woman simply as a toy. Now, I have never regarded woman as a toy. Woman is the intellectual helpmeet of man in public as in private life. Without her we should forget the true ideals.

Sits down beside LADY STUTFIELD

LADY STUTFIELD
I am so very, very glad to hear you say that.

LADY CAROLINE
You a married man, Mr Kettle?

SIR JOHN
Kelvil, dear, Kelvil.

KELVIL
I am married, Lady Caroline.

LADY CAROLINE
Family?

KELVIL
Yes.

LADY CAROLINE
How many?

325 *is it not?* at this point BLii, C, BLi, BLMS add the following exchange:

KELVIL
I have heard him speak with much levity about the sanctity of the marriage tie.

LADY S
That seems very, very wrong of him, does it not?

335–7 *Woman is the* . . . beside Lady Stutfield BLii, etc. (del. T; om. LC).

337 s.d. T, C (om. LC, etc.).

KELVIL
Eight.

LADY STUTFIELD *turns her attention to* LORD ALFRED

LADY CAROLINE
Mrs Kettle and the children are, I suppose, at the seaside?

SIR JOHN *shrugs his shoulders*

KELVIL
My wife is at the seaside with the children, Lady Caroline.

LADY CAROLINE
You will join them later on, no doubt?

KELVIL
If my public engagements permit me.

LADY CAROLINE
Your public life must be a great source of gratification to Mrs Kettle.

SIR JOHN
Kelvil, my love, Kelvil.

LADY STUTFIELD
(*To* LORD ALFRED) How very, very charming those gold-tipped cigarettes of yours are, Lord Alfred.

LORD ALFRED
They are awfully expensive. I can only afford them when I'm in debt.

LADY STUTFIELD
It must be terribly, terribly distressing to be in debt.

LORD ALFRED
One must have some occupation nowadays. If I hadn't my debts I shouldn't have anything to think about. All the chaps I know are in debt.

352–64 *Kelvil, my love . . . very strange* T, BLii, C (om. LC, BLi, BLMS).
360 *are in debt* at this point T adds the following exchange:

LADY S
I'm afraid you are sadly, sadly extravagant, Lord Alfred.

LORD A
I think if one can get a thing for ten shillings, it is absurd not to pay fifteen for it.

LADY S
How very, very strange!

Unpaid debts and cigarettes (preferably gold-tipped) were a favourite Wildean prop in both life and works. They reappear in a more emphatic form in *Earnest*, especially in the drafts for a sequence in which a solicitor arrives to arrest Algernon for debt.

LADY STUTFIELD
But don't the people to whom you owe the money give you a great, great deal of annoyance?

Enter FOOTMAN

LORD ALFRED
Oh no, they write; I don't.

LADY STUTFIELD
How very, very strange.

LADY HUNSTANTON
Ah, here is a letter, Caroline, from dear Mrs Arbuthnot. She won't dine. I am so sorry. But she will come in the evening. I am very pleased indeed. She is one of the sweetest of women. Writes a beautiful hand, too, so large, so firm.
Hands letter to LADY CAROLINE

LADY CAROLINE
(*Looking at it*) A little lacking in femininity, Jane. Femininity is the quality I admire most in women.

LADY HUNSTANTON
(*Taking back letter and leaving it on table*) Oh! she is very feminine, Caroline, and so good too. You should hear what the Archdeacon says of her. He regards her as his right hand in the parish. (FOOTMAN *speaks to her*) In the Yellow Drawing-room. Shall we all go in? Lady Stutfield, shall we go in to tea?

LADY STUTFIELD
With pleasure, Lady Hunstanton. *They rise and proceed to go off.* SIR JOHN *offers to carry* LADY STUTFIELD*'s cloak*

LADY CAROLINE
John! If you would allow your nephew to look after Lady Stutfield's cloak, you might help me with my workbasket.
Enter LORD ILLINGWORTH *and* MRS ALLONBY

SIR JOHN
Certainly, my love. *Exeunt*

MRS ALLONBY
Curious thing, plain women are always jealous of their husbands, beautiful women never are!

369–74 (Looking at it . . . *in the parish* (del. T; om. LC).
378–9 *If you would . . . workbasket* LC, T (om. BLii, etc).
381–3 *Curious thing . . . have time* T, etc. (om. LC).

LORD ILLINGWORTH

Beautiful women never have time. They are always so occupied in being jealous of other people's husbands.

MRS ALLONBY

I should have thought Lady Caroline would have grown tired of conjugal anxiety by this time! Sir John is her fourth!

LORD ILLINGWORTH

So much marriage is certainly not becoming. Twenty years of romance make a woman look like a ruin; but twenty years of marriage make her something like a public building.

MRS ALLONBY

Twenty years of romance! Is there such a thing?

LORD ILLINGWORTH

Not in our day. Women have become too brilliant. Nothing spoils a romance so much as a sense of humour in the woman.

MRS ALLONBY

Or the want of it in the man.

LORD ILLINGWORTH

You are quite right. In a Temple every one should be serious, except the thing that is worshipped.

MRS ALLONBY

And that should be man?

LORD ILLINGWORTH

Women kneel so gracefully; men don't.

MRS ALLONBY

You are thinking of Lady Stutfield!

383–4 *They are . . . people's husbands* (del. T; om. LC).

386 *Sir John is her fourth!* BLi and BLMS add following this line:

LORD I

Yes. I have often wondered what the others died of.

MRS AL

Fright, I should fancy.

391 *too brilliant* BLi and BLMS add here: 'and men too tedious;' the phrase is deleted in manuscript in BLi and omitted from BLii and subsequent drafts.

394 *Or the want of it in a man* originally (in BLi and BLMS) a part of Lord I's preceding speech. The redistribution of a speech among several characters is a common feature of Wilde's revisions.

398 *Women kneel so gracefully; men don't* LC, etc. (Women are so graceful when they kneel. Men aren't BLi, BLMS).

399–405 *You are . . . chief charm* T, BLii (om. LC, etc).

LORD ILLINGWORTH
I assure you I have not thought of Lady Stutfield for the last quarter of an hour.

MRS ALLONBY
Is she such a mystery?

LORD ILLINGWORTH
She is more than a mystery – she is a mood.

MRS ALLONBY
Moods don't last.

LORD ILLINGWORTH
It is their chief charm.

Enter HESTER *and* GERALD

GERALD
Lord Illingworth, every one has been congratulating me, Lady Hunstanton and Lady Caroline, and . . . every one. I hope I shall make a good secretary.

LORD ILLINGWORTH
You will be the pattern secretary, Gerald. *Talks to him*

MRS ALLONBY
You enjoy country life, Miss Worsley?

HESTER
Very much indeed.

MRS ALLONBY
Don't find yourself longing for a London dinner-party?

HESTER
I dislike London dinner-parties.

MRS ALLONBY
I adore them. The clever people never listen, and the stupid people never talk.

HESTER
I think the stupid people talk a great deal.

414–6 *The clever people . . . a great deal* a familiar opposition. Cf. *Earnest* I, 630–636:

JACK
I am sick to death of cleverness. Everybody is clever nowadays. You can't go anywhere without meeting clever people. The thing has become an absolute public nuisance. I wish to goodness we had a few fools left.

ALGERNON
We have.

JACK
I should like to meet them. What do they talk about?

ALGERNON
The fools? Oh! about the clever people, of course. (*CW*, p. 336.)

MRS ALLONBY
Ah, I never listen!

LORD ILLINGWORTH
My dear boy, if I didn't like you I wouldn't have made you the offer. It is because I like you so much that I want to have you with me. *Exit* HESTER *with* GERALD
Charming fellow, Gerald Arbuthnot!

MRS ALLONBY
He is very nice; very nice indeed. But I can't stand the American young lady.

LORD ILLINGWORTH
Why?

MRS ALLONBY
She told me yesterday, and in quite a loud voice too, that she was only eighteen. It was most annoying.

LORD ILLINGWORTH
One should never trust a woman who tells one her real age. A woman who would tell one that would tell one anything.

MRS ALLONBY
She is a Puritan besides –

LORD ILLINGWORTH
Ah, that is inexcusable. I don't mind plain women being Puritans. It is the only excuse they have for being plain. But she is decidedly pretty. I admire her immensely.
Looks steadfastly at MRS ALLONBY

MRS ALLONBY
What a thoroughly bad man you must be!

LORD ILLINGWORTH
What do you call a bad man?

418–19 *if I didn't . . . the offer* T, etc.
421 *Charming fellow, Gerald Arbuthnot* this line was originally part of a much larger series of exchanges. See Appendix I.
426 *only eighteen* the age for 'coming out' or entry into Society.
427–8 *One should never trust . . . anything* the theme of youth is common in Wilde's work and obsessed him during his life. He constantly lied about his own age. Youth is central to *Dorian Gray*. Cf. also *Earnest*, III, 249–51:

LADY BRACKNELL
Indeed, no woman should ever be quite accurate about her age. It looks so calculating. (*CW*, p. 376.)

429 *besides* — BLii, C, BLi, BLMS add here: 'an out and out Puritan — the worst I have ever met;' the extra words are deleted in manuscript in BLii and C.
430–1 *I don't mind . . . being plain* BLii, etc. (om. LC, T).
434 *What do you call* (What is? LC, etc.).

MRS ALLONBY
The sort of man who admires innocence.

LORD ILLINGWORTH
And a bad woman?

MRS ALLONBY
Oh! the sort of woman a man never gets tired of.

LORD ILLINGWORTH
You are severe – on yourself.

MRS ALLONBY
Define us as a sex.

LORD ILLINGWORTH
Sphinxes without secrets.

MRS ALLONBY
Does that include the Puritan women?

LORD ILLINGWORTH
Do you know, I don't believe in the existence of Puritan women? I don't think there is a woman in the world who would not be a little flattered if one made love to her. It is that which makes women so irresistibly adorable.

MRS ALLONBY
You think there is no woman in the world who would object to being kissed?

LORD ILLINGWORTH
Very few.

MRS ALLONBY
Miss Worsley would not let you kiss her.

LORD ILLINGWORTH
Are you sure?

436–7 *And a . . . tired of* LC, etc. (LORD I: And a bad woman is the sort of woman a man never gets tired of, isn't she BLi, BLMS).
439–40 *Define us . . . without secrets.* another quotation from *Dorian Gray*: 'Describe us as a sex,' was her challenge. 'Sphinxes without secrets.' (*DG*, p. 198/*CW*, p. 150.) 'The Sphinx' was Wilde's nickname for Ada Leverson. 'The Sphinx without a Secret' was the title of a short story in Wilde's collection *Lord Arthur Savile's Crime and Other Stories* (1891). Baudelaire's phrase (in an essay on Poe) for public opinion was 'ce sphinx sans énigme'.
442–5 *Do you know . . . adorable* in LC this speech is attributed to Lord Illingworth and not Lord Brancaster.
444 *made love to her* the older sense of the phrase — 'to pay court' or 'to woo' — is the one intended here.
446–8 *You think . . . Very few* LC, T, (om. BLii, etc.).

MRS ALLONBY
Quite.

LORD ILLINGWORTH
What do you think she'd do if I kissed her?

MRS ALLONBY
Either marry you, or strike you across the face with her glove. What would you do if she struck you across the face with her glove?

LORD ILLINGWORTH
Fall in love with her, probably.

MRS ALLONBY
Then it is lucky you are not going to kiss her!

LORD ILLINGWORTH
Is that a challenge?

MRS ALLONBY
It is an arrow shot into the air.

LORD ILLINGWORTH
Don't you know that I always succeed in whatever I try?

MRS ALLONBY
I am sorry to hear it. We women adore failures. They lean on us.

LORD ILLINGWORTH
You worship successes. You cling to them.

MRS ALLONBY
We are the laurels to hide their baldness.

LORD ILLINGWORTH
And they need you always, except at the moment of triumph.

MRS ALLONBY
They are uninteresting then.

LORD ILLINGWORTH
How tantalising you are! *A pause*

MRS ALLONBY
Lord Illingworth, there is one thing I shall always like you for.

452–7 *What do you . . . to kiss her!* see Appendix I.
458–9 *Is that . . . the air* LC, T (om. BLii, etc.).
460–7 *Don't you know . . . uninteresting then* T, etc. (om. LC).

LORD ILLINGWORTH
Only one thing? And I have so many bad qualities.

MRS ALLONBY
Ah, don't be too conceited about them. You may lose them as you grow old.

LORD ILLINGWORTH
I never intend to grow old. The soul is born old but grows young. That is the comedy of life.

MRS ALLONBY
And the body is born young and grows old. That is life's tragedy.

LORD ILLINGWORTH
Its comedy also, sometimes. But what is the mysterious reason why you will always like me?

MRS ALLONBY
It is that you have never made love to me.

LORD ILLINGWORTH
I have never done anything else.

MRS ALLONBY
Really? I have not noticed it.

LORD ILLINGWORTH
How fortunate! It might have been a tragedy for both of us.

MRS ALLONBY
We should each have survived.

LORD ILLINGWORTH
One can survive everything nowadays, except death, and live down anything except a good reputation.

MRS ALLONBY
Have you tried a good reputation?

LORD ILLINGWORTH
It is one of the many annoyances to which I have never been subjected.

MRS ALLONBY
It may come.

LORD ILLINGWORTH
Why do you threaten me?

478–83 *Its comedy . . . both of us* see Appendix I.
483 *tragedy for both of us* BLii, etc. (catastrophe for each of us, if you had T, LC).

MRS ALLONBY
I will tell you when you have kissed the Puritan.

Enter FOOTMAN

FRANCIS
Tea is served in the Yellow Drawing-room, my lord.

LORD ILLINGWORTH
Tell her ladyship we are coming in.

FRANCIS
Yes, my lord. *Exit*

LORD ILLINGWORTH
Shall we go in to tea?

MRS ALLONBY
Do you like such simple pleasures?

LORD ILLINGWORTH
I adore simple pleasures. They are the last refuge of the complex. But, if you wish, let us stay here. Yes, let us stay here. The Book of Life begins with a man and a woman in a garden.

MRS ALLONBY
It ends with Revelations.

LORD ILLINGWORTH
You fence divinely. But the button has come off your foil.

MRS ALLONBY
I have still the mask.

LORD ILLINGWORTH
It makes your eyes lovelier.

492 *the Puritan* BLii, C, BLi, BLMS add the following exchange after this speech:

LORD I
It will be this week, then.

MRS AL
I don't think so.

LORD I
You annoy me horribly, by saying so.

MRS AL
I see I do.

The lines are deleted in manuscript in BLii and C.

503–5 *You fence divinely . . . lovelier* another quotation from *Dorian Gray*:
'What are you looking for?' she enquired. 'The button from your foil,' he answered. 'You have dropped it.'
She laughed. 'I still have the mask.'
'It makes your eyes lovelier,' was the reply. (*DG*, p. 206/*CW*, p. 155.)

MRS ALLONBY

Thank you. Come.

LORD ILLINGWORTH

(*Sees* MRS ARBUTHNOT'*s letter on table, and takes it up and looks at envelope*) What a curious handwriting! It reminds me of the handwriting of a woman I used to know years ago.

MRS ALLONBY

Who?

LORD ILLINGWORTH

Oh! no one. No one in particular. A woman of no importance.

Throws letter down, and passes up the steps of the terrace with MRS ALLONBY. *They smile at each other*

ACT DROP

Second Act

Scene – Drawing-room at Hunstanton, after dinner, lamps lit. Door L.C. Door R.C. Ladies seated on sofas

MRS ALLONBY

What a comfort it is to have got rid of the men for a little!

LADY STUTFIELD

Yes; men persecute us dreadfully, don't they?

MRS ALLONBY

Persecute us? I wish they did.

LADY HUNSTANTON

My dear!

MRS ALLONBY

The annoying thing is that the wretches can be perfectly happy without us. That is why I think it is every woman's

510 *Oh! no one. No one in particular*. (om. LC, etc.).

511 s.d. (om. LC. [*Throws down letter.*] T, etc.).

s.d. BLMS adds '*Door at back opens on to terrace.*'

1 *for a little!* BLi, BLMS add to this speech: 'Really this is the only time during the twenty-four hours when one has any peace.' The sentence is deleted in manuscript in BLi.

4–12 *My dear . . . Hunstanton* BLii (del. Ti, Tii, Tiii; om. LC).

5 *The annoying thing is that* T, etc. (The annoying thing is that the wretches are so absolutely indifferent to us. Anyone who knows anything at all about men knows that C, BLi, BLMS).

duty never to leave them alone for a single moment, except during this short breathing space after dinner, without which I believe we poor women would be absolutely worn to shadows.

Enter SERVANTS *with coffee*

LADY HUNSTANTON
Worn to shadows, dear?

MRS ALLONBY
Yes, Lady Hunstanton. It is such a strain keeping men up to the mark. They are always trying to escape from us.

LADY STUTFIELD
It seems to me that it is we who are always trying to escape from them. Men are so very, very heartless. They know their power and use it.

LADY CAROLINE (*Takes coffee from* SERVANT)
What stuff and nonsense all this about men is! The thing to do is to keep men in their proper place.

MRS ALLONBY
But what is their proper place, Lady Caroline?

LADY CAROLINE
Looking after their wives, Mrs Allonby.

MRS ALLONBY (*Takes coffee from* SERVANT)
Really? And if they're not married?

LADY CAROLINE
If they are not married, they should be looking after a wife. It's perfectly scandalous the amount of bachelors who are

8 *this short breathing space after dinner* 'After the dessert wine has been passed once around the table, or about ten minutes after the servants have left the dining-room, the hostess should give the signal for the ladies to leave the dining-room [. . .]. The ladies on leaving the dining-room return to the drawing-room. Coffee should be almost immediately brought to the drawing-room. The coffee-cups containing coffee should be brought on a silver salver, with a cream-jug and a basin of crystallized sugar.' (*Manners and Rules of Good Society* [1888], p. 111.) This post-prandial segregation of the sexes varied between an hour (in the early decades of the century) to about fifteen minutes (in the '80s and '90s).

14–6 *It seems . . . use it* Tii, etc. (del. Tiii; om. LC).

18 *keep men in their proper place* a typical reversal of the accepted idea of the male roles that the play elsewhere assumes. Cf. Act II of *Earnest*:

GWENDOLEN
Outside the family circle, papa, I am glad to say, is entirely unknown. I think that is quite as it should be. The home seems to me to be the proper sphere for the man. (*Earnest*, II, 583-5/*CW*, p. 362.)

going about society. There should be a law passed to compel them all to marry within twelve months.

LADY STUTFIELD (*Refuses coffee*)
But if they're in love with someone who, perhaps, is tied to another?

LADY CAROLINE
In that case, Lady Stutfield, they should be married off in a week to some plain respectable girl, in order to teach them not to meddle with other people's property.

MRS ALLONBY
I don't think that we should ever be spoken of as other people's property. All men are married women's property. That is the only true definition of what married women's property really is. But we don't belong to any one.

LADY STUTFIELD
Oh, I am so very, very glad to hear you say so.

LADY HUNSTANTON
But do you really think, dear Caroline, that legislation would improve matters in any way? I am told that, nowadays, all the married men live like bachelors, and all the bachelors like married men.

MRS ALLONBY
I certainly never know one from the other.

LADY STUTFIELD
Oh, I think one can always know at once whether a man has home claims upon his life or not. I have noticed a very, very sad expression in the eyes of so many married men.

MRS ALLONBY
Ah, all that I have noticed is that they are horribly tedious

25 *twelve months* BLi and C have an additional sentence to this speech: 'I will certainly speak to that Mr Kettle on the subject.'
26 *someone who, perhaps* LC, etc. (someone whom they are not free to marry? Someone who C).
28–30 *In that case . . . people's property* BLii, etc. (They must be taught not to meddle with other people's property LC, Tiii). The reference is to the debate about legislation concerning married women's property. (There were two acts passed in the '80s and a third in 1893.)
36 *legislation* LC, etc. (such a law as you propose BLi, BLMS).
37–9 *I am told that . . . married men* another quotation from *Dorian Gray:* 'Nowadays all the married men live like bachelors, and all the bachelors like married men.' (*DG*, p. 179/*CW*, p. 137.) Cf. Lady Basildon's observation in *Husband*: 'Basildon . . . is as domestic as if he was a bachelor.' (I, 299–300.)
41–6 *Oh, I think . . . they are not* Tii, etc. (del. Tiii; om. LC).

when they are good husbands, and abominably conceited when they are not.

LADY HUNSTANTON
Well, I suppose the type of husband has completely changed since my young days, but I'm bound to state that poor dear Hunstanton was the most delightful of creatures, and as good as gold.

MRS ALLONBY
Ah, my husband is a sort of promissory note; I am tired of meeting him.

LADY CAROLINE
But you renew him from time to time, don't you?

MRS ALLONBY
Oh no, Lady Caroline. I have only had one husband as yet. I suppose you look upon me as quite an amateur.

LADY CAROLINE
With your views on life I wonder you married at all.

MRS ALLONBY
So do I.

LADY HUNSTANTON
My dear child, I believe you are really very happy in your married life, but that you like to hide your happiness from others.

MRS ALLONBY
I assure you I was horribly deceived in Ernest.

LADY HUNSTANTON
Oh, I hope not, dear. I knew his mother quite well. She was a Stratton, Caroline, one of Lord Crowland's daughters.

LADY CAROLINE
Victoria Stratton? I remember her perfectly. A silly fair-haired woman with no chin.

51 *promissory note* a document obliging the signatory to pay a stated sum to a particular person on a specified date or on demand; such debts were often capable of renegotiation or renewal.
53 *But you renew ... So do I* these lines are deleted in manuscript in Ti.
56–7 *With your views ... So do I* Tii, etc. (del. in Tiii; om. LC).
63 *Crowland* there were no Crowlands in the British peerage in 1893. Crowland is the name of a small town in Lincolnshire.

MRS ALLONBY
Ah, Ernest has a chin. He has a very strong chin, a square chin. Ernest's chin is far too square.

LADY STUTFIELD
But do you really think a man's chin can be too square? I think a man should look very, very strong, and that his chin should be quite, quite square.

MRS ALLONBY
Then you should certainly know Ernest, Lady Stutfield. It is only fair to tell you beforehand he has got no conversation at all.

LADY STUTFIELD
I adore silent men.

MRS ALLONBY
Oh, Ernest isn't silent. He talks the whole time. But he has got no conversation. What he talks about I don't know. I haven't listened to him for years.

LADY STUTFIELD
Have you never forgiven him then? How sad that seems! But all life is very, very sad, is it not?

MRS ALLONBY
Life, Lady Stutfield, is simply a *mauvais quart d'heure* made up of exquisite moments.

LADY STUTFIELD
Yes, there are moments, certainly. But was it something very, very wrong that Mr Allonby did? Did he become angry with you, and say anything that was unkind or true?

MRS ALLONBY
Oh dear, no. Ernest is invariably calm. That is one of the reasons he always gets on my nerves. Nothing is so aggravating as calmness. There is something positively brutal about the good temper of most modern men. I wonder we women stand it as well as we do.

66–7 *a very strong chin, a square chin* C, BLi, BLMS (a very square chin LC, Ti, Tii, Tiii, BLii).
74 *I adore silent men* before this line Tiii and LC have as a s.d. '(*Fanning herself*)'.
80 *mauvais quart d'heure* i.e. a bad quarter of an hour. At the end of his life Rossini is reputed to have told Emil Naumann, 'Monsieur Wagner a de beaux moments, mais de mauvais quarts d'heures aussi' ('M. Wagner has beautiful moments but bad quarters of an hour'; quoted in Francis Toye, *Rossini: A Study in Tragi-Comedy* [1934], p. 221). Rossini's comment was printed as an epigraph to H.W.L. Hime's *Wagnerism, A Protest* (1884).

LADY STUTFIELD
Yes; men's good temper shows they are not so sensitive as we are, not so finely strung. It makes a great barrier often between husband and wife, does it not? But I would so much like to know what was the wrong thing Mr Allonby did.

MRS ALLONBY
Well, I will tell you, if you solemnly promise to tell everybody else.

LADY STUTFIELD
Thank you, thank you. I will make a point of repeating it.

MRS ALLONBY
When Ernest and I were engaged he swore to me positively on his knees that he never had loved any one before in the whole course of his life. I was very young at the time, so I didn't believe him, I needn't tell you. Unfortunately, however, I made no enquiries of any kind till after I had been actually married four or five months. I found out then that what he had told me was perfectly true. And that sort of thing makes a man so absolutely uninteresting.

LADY HUNSTANTON
My dear!

MRS ALLONBY
Men always want to be a woman's first love. That is their clumsy vanity. We women have a more subtle instinct about things. What we like is to be a man's last romance.

LADY STUTFIELD
I see what you mean. It's very, very beautiful.

90–2 *Yes; men's . . . does it not?* (del. Tii, Tiii; om. LC).
BLi and BLMS have after this an additional speech for Lady C:
LADY C
It certainly would be a good thing if modern husbands lost their temper a little more often. They are far too easy going. They have no spirit.
The speech is deleted in manuscript in BLi. Cf. *Husband*, I, 294–310.

94–5 *if you solemnly . . . everybody else* (om. C, etc.).

96 *I will make . . . repeating it* (om. LC, etc.).

100–4 *Unfortunately . . . absolutely uninteresting* these are among some of the most heavily revised lines in the play. The fullest version — and the most laboured — is to be found in BLMS (later drafts progressively shorten the speech):
Unfortunately, however, not till after I had been actually married. I had been so occupied over my frocks that I had forgotten all about it, I suppose.
LADY S
And when you made careful enquiries you found —
MRS AL
Oh! I found it was perfectly true. He never *had* been in love with anyone else. And that sort of thing makes a man so absolutely uninteresting.

LADY HUNSTANTON
My dear child, you don't mean to tell me that you won't forgive your husband because he never loved any one else? Did you ever hear such a thing, Caroline? I am quite surprised.

LADY CAROLINE
Oh, women have become so highly educated, Jane, that nothing should surprise us nowadays, except happy marriages. They apparently are getting remárkably rare.

MRS ALLONBY
Oh, they're quite out of date.

LADY STUTFIELD
Except amongst the middle classes, I have been told.

MRS ALLONBY
How like the middle classes!

LADY STUTFIELD
Yes – is it not? – very, very like them.

LADY CAROLINE
If what you tell us about the middle classes is true, Lady Stutfield, it redounds greatly to their credit. It is much to be regretted that in our rank of life the wife should be so persistently frivolous, under the impression apparently that it is the proper thing to be. It is to that I attribute the unhappiness of so many marriages we all know of in society.

MRS ALLONBY
Do you know, Lady Caroline, I don't think the frivolity of the wife has ever anything to do with it. More marriages are ruined nowadays by the common sense of the husband than by anything else. How can a woman be expected to be happy with a man who insists on treating her as if she were a perfectly rational being?

LADY HUNSTANTON
My dear!

MRS ALLONBY
Man, poor, awkward, reliable, necessary man belongs to a sex that has been rational for millions and millions of years. He

110–11 *My dear child . . . any one else* (del. Tiii; om. LC).
114 *women have . . . Jane, that* (del. Ti, Tii, Tiii; om. LC).
121–7 *If what you . . . in society* BLii (It is when wives become frivolous that marriages become unhappy Tiii, LC).
136 *millions and millions* BLii, C, BLi, BLMS (millions LC, etc.).

can't help himself. It is in his race. The History of Woman is very different. We have always been picturesque protests against the mere existence of common sense. We saw its dangers from the first.

LADY STUTFIELD
Yes, the common sense of husbands is certainly most, most trying. Do tell me your conception of the Ideal Husband. I think it would be so very, very helpful.

MRS ALLONBY
The Ideal Husband? There couldn't be such a thing. The institution is wrong.

LADY STUTFIELD
The Ideal Man, then, in his relations to *us*.

LADY CAROLINE
He would probably be extremely realistic.

MRS ALLONBY
The Ideal Man! Oh, the Ideal Man should talk to us as if we were goddesses, and treat us as if we were children. He should refuse all our serious requests, and gratify every one of our whims. He should encourage us to have caprices, and forbid us to have missions. He should always say much more than he means, and always mean much more than he says.

LADY HUNSTANTON
But how could he do both, dear?

MRS ALLONBY
He should never run down other pretty women. That would show he had no taste, or make one suspect that he had too much. No; he should be nice about them all, but say that somehow they don't attract him.

137 *his race* here BLMS adds: 'The caveman began it, in order to annoy his wife, I have no doubt.' The line deleted in manuscript in BLi.

144–5 *The institution is wrong* BLMS and BLi add the following exchange here:

LADY S
The ideal man, then. Tell us about him.

LADY H
Oh, I hope the ideal man won't appear. If he were brought out, there would be too many applications for shares.

147 *extremely realistic* at this point BLMS has an additional speech for Lady S: 'Won't you tell us, Mrs Allenby. You seem to have studied this subject so very, very earnestly.'
The speech is deleted in manuscript in BLi, but Wilde's intention to present Mrs Al as an authority on contemporary conduct is preserved in a s.d. to Tiii: '*(Foot on stool)*'.

155–7 *That would show ... too much* (del. Tiii; om. LC).

LADY STUTFIELD

Yes, that is always very, very pleasant to hear about other women.

MRS ALLONBY

If we ask him a question about anything, he should give us an answer all about ourselves. He should invariably praise us for whatever qualities he knows we haven't got. But he should be pitiless, quite pitiless, in reproaching us for the virtues that we have never dreamed of possessing. He should never believe that we know the use of useful things. That would be unforgiveable. But he should shower on us everything we don't want.

LADY CAROLINE

As far as I can see, he is to do nothing but pay bills and compliments.

MRS ALLONBY

He should persistently compromise us in public, and treat us with absolute respect when we are alone. And yet he should be always ready to have a perfectly terrible scene, whenever we want one, and to become miserable, absolutely miserable, at a moment's notice, and to overwhelm us with just reproaches in less than twenty minutes, and to be positively violent at the end of half an hour, and to leave us for ever at a quarter to eight, when we have to go and dress for dinner. And when, after that, one has seen him for really the last time, and he has refused to take back the little things he has given one, and promised never to communicate with one again, or to write one any foolish letters, he should be perfectly broken-hearted, and telegraph to one all day long, and send one little notes every half-hour by a private hansome, and dine quite alone at the club, so that every one should know how unhappy he was. And after a whole dreadful week, during which one has gone about everywhere with one's husband, just to show how absolutely lonely one was, he may be given

165 *possessing* here BLMS and BLi have additional lines:
'To be called heartless is charming when one has a heart. And to be reproached as a dragon of virtue is exquisite if one happens to be in a romantic mood.'
The phrase 'dragon of good taste' is used in *Husband*, I, 244–5.

165–7 *He should . . . unforgiveable* LC, etc. (om. Ti).

170 *compliments* see Appendix I.

175–6 *and to overwhelm . . . twenty minutes* (del. Ti, Tii, Tiii; om. LC).

184–5 *dine quite alone at the club* the allusion here is to the powerful effect of ostracism in nineteenth-century society. Cf. Lord Fermor's remarks about Lord Kelso in *Dorian Gray*: 'The thing was hushed up, but, egad, Kelso ate his chop alone at the club for some time afterwards,' (*DG*, p. 33/*CW*, p. 39), and the ostracism of Dorian himself later in the novel.

a third last parting, in the evening, and then, if his conduct has been quite irreproachable, and one has behaved really badly to him, he should be allowed to admit that he has been entirely in the wrong, and when he has admitted that, it becomes a woman's duty to forgive, and one can do it all over again from the beginning, with variations.

LADY HUNSTANTON

How clever you are, my dear! You never mean a single word you say.

LADY STUTFIELD

Thank you, thank you. It has been quite, quite entrancing. I must try and remember it all. There are such a number of details that are so very, very important.

LADY CAROLINE

But you have not told us yet what the reward of the Ideal Man is to be.

MRS ALLONBY

His reward? Oh, infinite expectation. That is quite enough for him.

LADY STUTFIELD

But men are so terribly, terribly exacting, are they not?

MRS ALLONBY

That makes no matter. One should never surrender.

LADY STUTFIELD

Not even to the Ideal Man?

MRS ALLONBY

Certainly not to him. Unless, of course, one wants to grow tired of him.

LADY STUTFIELD

Oh! . . . yes. I see that. It is very, very helpful. Do you think, Mrs Allonby, I shall ever meet the Ideal Man? Or are there more than one?

MRS ALLONBY

There are just four in London, Lady Stutfield.

192 *admitted that* LC, etc. (admitted that, and looks very pale and sad and worn under the eyes C).
197 *It has been quite, quite entrancing* BLii, BLi, (om. LC, etc.).
198–9 *I must try . . . very important* (del Tiii; om. LC).
204–9 *But men are . . . helpful* Ti, BLii, C, BLi, BLMS (del. Tii, Tiii; om. LC).
212 *Lady Stutfield* see Appendix I.

LADY HUNSTANTON
Oh, my dear!

MRS ALLONBY (*Going over to her*)
What has happened? Do tell me.

LADY HUNSTANTON (*In a low voice*)
I had completely forgotten that the American young lady has been in the room all the time. I am afraid some of this clever talk may have shocked her a little.

MRS ALLONBY
Ah, that will do her so much good!

LADY HUNSTANTON
Let us hope she didn't understand much. I think I had better go over and talk to her. (*Rises and goes across to* HESTER WORSLEY) Well, dear Miss Worsley. (*Sitting down beside her*) How quiet you have been in your nice little corner all this time! I suppose you have been reading a book? There are so many books here in the library.

HESTER
No, I have been listening to the conversation.

LADY HUNSTANTON
You mustn't believe everything that was said, you know, dear.

HESTER
I didn't believe any of it.

LADY HUNSTANTON
That is quite right, dear.

HESTER (*Continuing*)
I couldn't believe that any women could really hold such views of life as I have heard tonight from some of your guests.

An awkward pause

LADY HUNSTANTON
I hear you have such pleasant society in America. Quite like

216 *time* here BLMS has an additional speech for Mrs Al:

MRS AL
Had you really? Oh, I knew she was here, Lady Hunstanton. One can't help noticing her, she is so simply dressed.

The speech is deleted in manuscript in BLi.

216–7 *this clever talk* (us LC, Ti, Tiii, C).

219–21 *I think . . . dear Miss Worsley* see Appendix I.

223–4 *There are so many books here in the library* BLii, etc. (del. Tii, om. LC).

231 *your guests* see Appendix I.

our own in places, my son wrote to me.

HESTER

There are cliques in America as elsewhere, Lady Hunstanton. But true American society consists simply of all the good women and good men we have in our country.

LADY HUNSTANTON

What a sensible system, and I dare say quite pleasant too. I am afraid in England we have too many artificial social barriers. We don't see as much as we should of the middle and lower classes.

HESTER

In America we have no lower classes.

LADY HUNSTANTON

Really? What a very strange arrangement!

MRS ALLONBY

What is that dreadful girl talking about?

LADY STUTFIELD

She is painfully natural, is she not?

LADY CAROLINE

There are a great many things you haven't got in America, I am told, Miss Worsley. They say you have no ruins, and no curiosities.

MRS ALLONBY (*To* LADY STUTFIELD)

What nonsense! They have their mothers and their manners.

HESTER

The English aristocracy supply us with our curiosities, Lady Caroline. They are sent over to us every summer, regularly, in the steamers, and propose to us the day after they land. As for ruins, we are trying to build up something that will last longer than brick or stone.

Gets up to take her fan from table

233 *wrote to me* BLii, etc. (told me LC, Ti, Tii, Tiii).

234 *Lady Hunstanton* C, BLi, BLMS add here:

and money is thought far too much of there, as it is here, and we also have foolish people who pride themselves on the accident of family and birth. But they are of no real importance with us.

Like Hester's other criticisms of the divisive nature of British society, these lines were omitted from all the later drafts of the play and from LC.

243 *What is . . . talking about* BLii, C (del. Ti, Tii, Tiii; om. LC). BLi and BLMS add: 'I have not heard a word she has said.'

248 *mothers* (parents, T, etc.). Mrs Al's whole speech is omitted from LC.

LADY HUNSTANTON
What is that, dear? Ah, yes, an iron Exhibition, is it not, at that place that has the curious name?

HESTER (*Standing by table*)
We are trying to build up life, Lady Hunstanton, on a better, truer, purer basis than life rests on here. This sounds strange to you all, no doubt. How could it sound other than strange? You rich people in England, you don't know how you are living. How could you know? You shut out from your society the gentle and the good. You laugh at the simple and the pure. Living, as you all do, on others and by them, you sneer at self-sacrifice, and if you throw bread to the poor, it is merely to keep them quiet for a season. With all your pomp and wealth and art you don't know how to live – you don't even know that. You love the beauty that you can see and touch and handle, the beauty that you can destroy, and do destroy, but of the unseen beauty of life, of the unseen beauty of a higher life, you know nothing. You have lost life's secret. Oh, your English society seems to me shallow, selfish, foolish. It has blinded its eyes, and stopped its ears. It lies like a leper in purple. It sits like a dead thing smeared with gold. It is all wrong, all wrong.

LADY STUTFIELD
I don't think one should know of these things. It is not very, very nice, is it?

255–6 *an iron Exhibition . . . curious name* a reference to the International Exhibition or World's Fair held at Jackson Park, Chicago from May to November 1893. The Machinery Hall was constructed mainly of iron and glass and was thought by some to resemble British railway stations. Wilde knew of the Fair in September, 1892 (see *Letters*, p. 320), and expected that the play would be performed there.

258 *here* BLMS adds:

We are trying to reconstruct society on other foundations than those of luxury and pride, of selfishness and sin. For it is sin that allows others to starve that it may surfeit and lives in idleness itself on the work of weak hands and the toil of wretched days.

The lines are deleted in manuscript in BLi. The first sentence is kept in BLii, Ti, Tii, Tiii, but omitted in LC.

263–5 *Living . . . for a season* (del. Ti, Tiii; om. LC). Following the sentence C, BLi, BLMS add:

You cultivated people in England don't know *why* you are living. You never think of *that*. Think of it sometimes. What does your wealth give you but weariness? What do your pleasures bring you but *ennui* and pain? There are more haggard faces in a London Drawing room than you will find in the most sunless lane of your great, unjust city, more haggard faces, and more aching hearts.

266 *wealth and art* LC, etc. (riches BLMS).

271 *selfish, foolish* here BLMS adds: 'It counts nothing holy, nothing sacred.'

274 *wrong, all wrong* at this point BLMS has an additional speech for Mrs Al:

What bad form to talk like that.

The speech is deleted in manuscript in BLi.

LADY HUNSTANTON

My dear Miss Worsley, I thought you liked English society so much. You were such a success in it. And you were so much admired by the best people. I quite forget what Lord Henry Weston said of you – but it was most complimentary, and you know what an authority he is on beauty.

HESTER

Lord Henry Weston! I remember him, Lady Hunstanton. A man with a hideous smile and a hideous past. He is asked everywhere. No dinner-party is complete without him. What of those whose ruin is due to him? They are outcasts. They are nameless. If you met them in the street you would turn your head away. I don't complain of their punishment. Let all women who have sinned be punished.

MRS ARBUTHNOT *enters from terrace behind in a cloak with lace veil over her head. She hears the last words and starts*

LADY HUNSTANTON

My dear young lady!

HESTER

It is right that they should be punished, but don't let them be the only ones to suffer. If a man and woman have sinned, let them both go forth into the desert to love or loathe each other there. Let them both be branded. Set a mark, if you wish, on each, but don't punish the one and let the other go free. Don't have one law for men and another for women. You are unjust to women in England. And till you count what is a shame in a woman to be an infamy in a man, you will always

278 *success in it* BLMS adds here:
Why, you went everywhere last season, didn't you? The papers were full of your doings.
The lines are deleted in BLi.

280 *Weston* a title extinct since 1688.

283–7 *hideous past ... punishment* these lines are much fuller in BLMS:
A man who, I am told, has brought many women to misery and to shame. A man who has wrecked innocent lives, and poisoned lives that were pure. *He* is asked everywhere. No dinner party is complete without him. To have him in one's box at the Opera is a distinction. To be on his drag in the Park an honour. What of the women whose ruin is *due* to *him? They* are outcasts. *They* are nameless. If you met *them* in the street you would turn your head away. Their own families forget them. Those who had received kindnesses from them pass them by. I don't complain of their punishment.

293 *other there* BLMS adds here:
and there be bound together in their shame as they were in their madness.

295 *one law for men and another for women* the idea of different social and legal codes for men and women was intensely topical and had formed a major part of *LWF*. (Cf. the comic use of the phrase in *Earnest*, III, 408-410.)

be unjust, and Right, that pillar of fire, and Wrong, that pillar of cloud, will be made dim to your eyes, or be not seen at all, or if seen, not regarded.

LADY CAROLINE

Might I, dear Miss Worsley, as you are standing up, ask you for my cotton that is just behind you? Thank you.

LADY HUNSTANTON

My dear Mrs Arbuthnot! I am so pleased you have come up. But I didn't hear you announced.

MRS ARBUTHNOT

Oh, I came straight in from the terrace, Lady Hunstanton, just as I was. You didn't tell me you had a party.

LADY HUNSTANTON

Not a party. Only a few guests who are staying in the house, and whom you must know. Allow me. (*Tries to help her. Rings bell*) Caroline, this is Mrs Arbuthnot, one of my sweetest friends. Lady Caroline Pontefract, Lady Stutfield, Mrs Allonby, and my young American friend, Miss Worsley, who has just been telling us all how wicked we are.

HESTER

I am afraid you think I spoke too strongly, Lady Hunstanton. But there are some things in England –

LADY HUNSTANTON

My dear young lady, there was a great deal of truth, I dare

298–9 *pillar of fire . . . pillar of cloud* from *Exodus* 13.21:
'And the Lord went before them by day in a pillar of cloud, to lead them the way; and by night in a pillar of fire, to give them light.'
The idea of emigration to a better life is picked up in Act IV. See Introduction.

301–2 *Might I . . . Thank you* one of Wilde's most famous *coups de théâtre*, this speech was in fact an afterthought to BLMS.

304 *announced* BLMS adds here:
Miss Worsley has been talking to us in such an interesting manner, I am afraid you must have thought me quite rude.
(The rudeness in fact is Hester's, hence Lady H's emphasis on strict social propriety.) 'Announcing' was the means of formally welcoming new arrivals to a party or dinner. At large gatherings the butler, stationed on the staircase, would announce guests. On less elaborate occasions the onus was on the guests to give their names to a servant to announce them. The confusion here points to Mrs A's social naivety.

306 *had a party* Ti, Tii, Tiii add a s.d.:
(*Hester hands a reel of cotton to Lady C, who bows*)
Lady C's coldness here emphasises the tension over etiquette. A 'party' would imply a formal and invited (although not necessarily large) gathering.

310 *Pontefract* BLi, etc. (Stanford BLMS).

314 *But there . . . England* (del. Ti, Tii, Tiii; om. LC; But there are some things I feel very deeply about, and I have been very foolish perhaps BLMS).

say, in what you said, and you looked very pretty while you said it, which is much more important, Lord Illingworth would tell us. The only point where I thought you were a little hard was about Lady Caroline's brother, about poor Lord Henry. He is really such good company.

Enter FOOTMAN

Take Mrs Arbuthnot's things.

Exit FOOTMAN *with wraps*

HESTER

Lady Caroline, I had no idea it was your brother. I am sorry for the pain I must have caused you – I –

LADY CAROLINE

My dear Miss Worsley, the only part of your little speech, if I may so term it, with which I thoroughly agreed, was the part about my brother. Nothing that you could possibly say could be too bad for him. I regard Henry as infamous, absolutely infamous. But I am bound to state, as you were remarking, Jane, that he is excellent company, and he has one of the best cooks in London, and after a good dinner one can forgive anybody, even one's own relations.

LADY HUNSTANTON (*To* MISS WORSLEY)

Now, do come, dear, and make friends with Mrs Arbuthnot. She is one of the good, sweet, simple people you told us we never admitted into society. I am sorry to say Mrs Arbuthnot comes very rarely to me. But that is not my fault.

MRS ALLONBY

What a bore it is the men staying so long after dinner! I expect they are saying the most dreadful things about us.

LADY STUTFIELD

Do you really think so?

MRS ALLONBY

I am sure of it.

321 s.d. ([*Exit* FOOTMAN *with wraps*] BLi; [*Exit* FOOTMAN *with wraps*. LADY H *and* MRS AR *sit down on sofa*] Ti, Tii, Tiii, BLii).

325 *so term it* (call it so C, etc.).

332–5 *Now, do come . . . not my fault* (del. T; om. LC). This part of the act is much revised in all versions. BLi and BLMS add to the end of Lady H's speech:

We go to her, and her tea is much better than mine, and she makes us all feel very good, which is a pleasant thing.

LADY STUTFIELD

How very, very horrid of them! Shall we go on to the terrace?

MRS ALLONBY

Oh, anything to get away from the dowagers and the dowdies. (*Rises and goes with* LADY STUTFIELD *to door L.C.*) We are only going to look at the stars, Lady Hunstanton.

LADY HUNSTANTON

You will find a great many, dear, a great many. But don't catch cold. (*To* MRS ARBUTHNOT) We shall all miss Gerald so much, dear Mrs Arbuthnot.

MRS ARBUTHNOT

But has Lord Illingworth really offered to make Gerald his secretary?

LADY HUNSTANTON

Oh, yes! He has been most charming about it. He has the highest possible opinion of your boy. You don't know Lord Illingworth, I believe, dear.

340–4 *How very, very . . . Lady Hunstanton* in BLi and BLMS this exchange is much fuller:

LADY S

How very, very horrid of them.

MRS AL

I wish to goodness they would come. It is horribly selfish of them leaving us here like this.

LADY S

Yes, horribly, horribly selfish. Shall we go on to the terrace?

MRS AL

Oh, anything to get away from the dowagers and the dowdies.

Rises and goes with Lady S to door at back opening on to terrace

LADY S

I don't very, very much like that American girl.

MRS AL

I can't stand her. I don't mind plain people being Puritans. It is the only excuse they have for being plain. But she is undoubtedly pretty and should know better. We are only going to look at the stars, Lady Hunstanton.

Mrs Al's final speech here is deleted in BLi and moved to Act I, 430–1 in subsequent drafts. For another reference to 'dowdies', cf. *Husband*, I, 320.

346 *We shall all miss* preceding this sentence BLi and BLMS have an additional exchange:

LADY H

Miss Worsley and Aleck are fast friends, dear Mrs Arbuthnot.

MABEL

Your son has been very kind to me, during my stay here.

MRS AR

Aleck has spoken to me about you several times. He is so pleased to have had the honour of meeting you.

348–52 *But has Lord . . . dear* see Appendix I.

MRS ARBUTHNOT
I have never met him.

LADY HUNSTANTON
You know him by name, no doubt?

MRS ARBUTHNOT
I am afraid I don't. I live so much out of the world, and see so few people. I remember hearing years ago of an old Lord Illingworth who lived in Yorkshire, I think.

LADY HUNSTANTON
Ah, yes. That would be the last Earl but one. He was a very curious man. He wanted to marry beneath him. Or wouldn't, I believe. There was some scandal about it. The present Lord Illingworth is quite different. He is very distinguished. He does – well, he does nothing, which I am afraid our pretty American visitor here thinks very wrong of anybody, and I don't know that he cares much for the subjects in which you are so interested, dear Mrs Arbuthnot. Do you think, Caroline, that Lord Illingworth is interested in the Housing of the Poor?

LADY CAROLINE
I should fancy not at all, Jane.

LADY HUNSTANTON
We all have our different tastes, have we not? But Lord Illingworth has a very high position, and there is nothing he couldn't get if he chose to ask for it. Of course, he is comparatively a young man still, and he has only come to his title within – how long exactly is it, Caroline, since Lord Illingworth succeeded?

LADY CAROLINE
About four years, I think, Jane. I know it was the same year

353 *I have never met him.* LC, Ti, Tii, Tiii, BLii add: 'But I am sure to like anyone who is kind to Gerald.'
362–3 *which I am afraid . . . wrong of anybody* (del. Ti; om. LC).
370–1 *has a very . . . Of course* (del. Ti; om. LC).
370 *high position* T, etc. (high position and great wealth BLi, BLMS).
371 *ask for it* here BLMS has in addition:
I fancy, Caroline, that Diplomacy is what Lord Illingworth is aiming at. I have heard it said he wanted Vienna, but that may not be true.
This part of the speech was deleted in BLi and moved to I, 85–7.

in which my brother had his last exposure in the evening newspapers.

LADY HUNSTANTON
Ah, I remember. That would be about four years ago. Of course, there were a great many people between the present Lord Illingworth and the title, Mrs Arbuthnot. There was – who was there, Caroline?

LADY CAROLINE
There was poor Margaret's baby. You remember how anxious she was to have a boy, and it was a boy, but it died, and her husband died shortly afterwards, and she married almost immediately one of Lord Ascot's sons, who, I am told, beats her.

LADY HUNSTANTON
Ah, that is in the family, dear, that is in the family. And there was also, I remember, a clergyman who wanted to be a lunatic, or a lunatic who wanted to be a clergyman, I forget which, but I know the Court of Chancery investigated the matter, and decided that he was quite sane. And I saw him afterwards at poor Lord Plumstead's with straws in his hair, or something very odd about him. I can't recall what. I often regret, Lady Caroline, that dear Lady Cecilia never lived to see her son get the title.

MRS ARBUTHNOT
Lady Cecilia?

LADY HUNSTANTON
Lord Illingworth's mother, dear Mrs Arbuthnot, was one of

376–7 *evening newspapers* here BLMS has in addition:
for we had to give up taking the newspapers for a long time. They made what they called a 'moral example' of him. And naturally it was impossible for any respectable person even to glance at them, while they were doing that.
Cf. 'Lord Arthur Savile's Crime': 'He hated the idea of being lionised at Lady Windermere's, or seeing his name figuring in the paragraphs of vulgar society newspapers.' (*CSF*, p. 34/*CW*, p. 179.) The papers Lady C refers to would have been the *St. James Gazette*, the *Pall Mall Gazette*, the *Echo*, the *Evening News*, and the *Globe*.

385 *Ascot* LC, etc (Royston C, BLi, BLMS) The Royston baronetcy became extinct in 1708; there was no Ascot title in the British peerage in 1893.

387 *family* here BLMS adds:
Then there was that young man, a great friend of my son's. I have forgotten his Christian name, another of the Harbords of course, they're such a very large family, who . . . It was a sad case altogether.

392 *Plumstead* there was no such title in the British peerage; Plumstead is the name of a village in Norfolk.

392 *with straws in his hair* a traditional sign of madness.

397 *Lord Illingworth's mother* BLMS names her as 'Lady Cecilia Harleston'.

the Duchess of Jerningham's pretty daughters, and she married Sir Thomas Harford, who wasn't considered a very good match for her at the time, though he was said to be the handsomest man in London. I knew them all quite intimately, and both the sons, Arthur and George.

MRS ARBUTHNOT

It was the eldest son who succeeded, of course, Lady Hunstanton?

LADY HUNSTANTON

No, dear, he was killed in the hunting field. Or was it fishing, Caroline? I forget. But George came in for everything. I always tell him that no younger son has ever had such good luck as he has had.

MRS ARBUTHNOT

Lady Hunstanton, I want to speak to Gerald at once. Might I see him? Can he be sent for?

LADY HUNSTANTON

Certainly, dear. I will send one of the servants into the dining-room to fetch him. I don't know what keeps the gentlemen so long. (*Rings bell*) When I knew Lord Illingworth first as plain George Harford, he was simply a very brilliant young man about town, with not a penny of money except what poor dear Lady Cecilia gave him. She was quite devoted to him. Chiefly, I fancy, because he was on bad terms with his father. Oh, here is the dear Archdeacon. (*To* SERVANT) It doesn't matter.

399 *Sir Thomas Harford* the name of Lord I's father changes through the drafts. See 'The Play, Its Drafts and Genesis'.

401 *in London* LC, etc. (in London. However, he came in almost immediately for all the Renton property, so that they were very comfortably off, though I remember, Caroline, poor dear Lady Cecilia always complained of being poor, but that was long afterwards when they didn't get on very well together.' C, etc.).

403 *It was the* LC, Ti, Tii, Tiii, BLii have Lady S and Mrs Al enter immediately before this speech.

406 *for everything* BLMS adds following this sentence:

the baronetcy, and the peerage, and the Illingworth estates, so far as they were entailed. I believe a good deal of it was left away in an odd manner. But George got his slice, and the house in St. James's Square, and goodness knows what else.

413–9 *When I knew . . . It doesn't matter* (del. Ti; om. LC).

416 *Lady Cecilia gave him* T, etc. (Lady Cecilia gave him. She spoiled him quite dreadfully, I am bound to state. She was quite devoted to him. BLMS).

417–8 *with his father* see Appendix I.

419 s.d. LC, Ti, Tii, Tiii, BLii have an entrance for Mr K with Sir J and Dr D.

Enter SIR JOHN *and* DOCTOR DAUBENY. SIR JOHN *goes over to* LADY STUTFIELD, DOCTOR DAUBENY *to* LADY HUNSTANTON

THE ARCHDEACON
Lord Illingworth has been most entertaining. I have never enjoyed myself more. (*Sees* MRS ARBUTHNOT) Ah, Mrs Arbuthnot.

LADY HUNSTANTON (*To* DOCTOR DAUBENY)
You see I have got Mrs Arbuthnot to come to me at last.

THE ARCHDEACON
That is a great honour, Lady Hunstanton. Mrs Daubeny will be quite jealous of you.

LADY HUNSTANTON
Ah, I am so sorry Mrs Daubeny could not come with you tonight. Headache as usual, I suppose?

THE ARCHDEACON
Yes, Lady Hunstanton; a perfect martyr. But she is happiest alone. She is happiest alone.

LADY CAROLINE (*To her husband*)
John! SIR JOHN *goes over to his wife*

DOCTOR DAUBENY *talks to* LADY HUNSTANTON *and* MRS ARBUTHNOT

MRS ARBUTHNOT *watches* LORD ILLINGWORTH *the whole time. He has passed across the room without noticing her, and approaches* MRS ALLONBY, *who with* LADY STUTFIELD *is standing by the door looking on to the terrace*

LORD ILLINGWORTH
How is the most charming woman in the world?

MRS ALLONBY (*Taking* LADY STUTFIELD *by the hand*)
We are both quite well, thank you, Lord Illingworth. But what a short time you have been in the dining-room! It seems as if we had only just left.

LORD ILLINGWORTH
I was bored to death. Never opened my lips the whole time.

430 *John!* BLi, etc. (John! SIR J: Yes, my love! LC, Ti, Tii, Tiii, BLii). At this point LC announces Lord I's entrance.
432–43 *But what . . . give me?* (del. Ti, Tiii; om. LC).
434 *left* BLi and BLMS add here: 'You might have waited for another cigarette', so reinforcing the relationship between advanced habits (liking smoking) and emancipation that the first drafts of the play establish.

Absolutely longing to come in to you.

MRS ALLONBY
You should have. The American girl has been giving us a lecture.

LORD ILLINGWORTH
Really? All Americans lecture, I believe. I suppose it is something in their climate. What did she lecture about?

MRS ALLONBY
Oh, Puritanism, of course.

LORD ILLINGWORTH
I am going to convert her, am I not? How long do you give me?

MRS ALLONBY
A week.

LORD ILLINGWORTH
A week is more than enough.

Enter GERALD *and* LORD ALFRED

GERALD (*Going to* MRS ARBUTHNOT)
Dear mother!

MRS ARBUTHNOT
Gerald, I don't feel at all well. See me home, Gerald. I shouldn't have come.

GERALD
I am so sorry, mother. Certainly. But you must know Lord Illingworth first.

Goes across room

MRS ARBUTHNOT
Not tonight, Gerald.

439 *All Americans lecture* lecture tours were (and remain) a popular and profitable form of public instruction in the United States. Wilde himself undertook such a tour in the winter of 1881.

444–5 *A week . . . more than enough* here Ti has a manuscript note 'I don't think so' and these lines are deleted in manuscript and omitted in LC, an indication that T could have been the copy text for LC.

466 *Dear mother!* LC, etc. ([*to* MABEL] How unkind of Lady Hunstanton not putting me next to you at dinner. [*Going to* MRS AR] Dear mother, I am so delighted you have come up. BLi, BLMS).

GERALD

Lord Illingworth, I want you so much to know my mother.

LORD ILLINGWORTH

With the greatest pleasure. (*To* MRS ALLONBY) I'll be back in a moment. People's mothers always bore me to death. All women become like their mothers. That is their tragedy.

MRS ALLONBY

No man does. That is his.

LORD ILLINGWORTH

What a delightful mood you are in tonight!

Turns round and goes across with GERALD *to* MRS ARBUTHNOT. *When he sees her, he starts back in wonder. Then slowly his eyes turn towards* GERALD

GERALD

Mother, this is Lord Illingworth, who has offered to take me as his private secretary. (MRS ARBUTHNOT *bows coldly*) It is a wonderful opening for me, isn't it? I hope he won't be disappointed in me, that is all. You'll thank Lord Illingworth, mother, won't you?

MRS ARBUTHNOT

Lord Illingworth is very good, I am sure, to interest himself in you for the moment.

LORD ILLINGWORTH (*Putting his hand on* GERALD'*s shoulder*)

Oh, Gerald and I are great friends already, Mrs ... Arbuthnot.

452 *Lord Illingworth, I want you so much to know my mother* BLii, etc. (Oh, do speak to him for a moment. It is so important for me. Lord Illingworth, I want you so much to know my mother LC, Ti, Tii, Tiii; Lord Illingworth, I want you so much to know my mother. She has come up specially to meet you and she has to go away almost at once BLi, BLMS).

454–5 *All women ... tragedy* in all drafts these lines are given to Mrs Al. Cf. Algernon in *Earnest*: 'All women become like their mothers. That is their tragedy. No man does. That's his.' (*Earnest*, I, 625-6/*CW*, p. 335.)

457 s.d. Tii and Tiii have additional directions which emphasise the idea of a struggle for Gerald. After l. 462 Tiii has '(ILL *touches* GERALD)' and at the end of l. 466 Tiii and Tii have '(MRS ARBUTHNOT *puts hand on* GERALD)'.

461 *that is all* here BLi and BLMS add:

I am sorry now I didn't work harder when I was at school. But I must try and make up for lost time now, mustn't I, mother?

465–6 *Mrs ... Arbuthnot* Tii typescript ends here. BLi, BLMS add:

You don't mind my calling you Aleck, I know.

ALECK

Oh, I think it is very nice of you, Lord Illingworth. Everyone somehow, calls me Aleck. I sometimes forget my name is Arbuthnot.

LORD I

I can quite understand it. I took a great fancy to your son the moment I met

MRS ARBUTHNOT

There can be nothing in common between you and my son, Lord Illingworth.

GERALD

Dear mother, how can you say so? Of course, Lord Illingworth is awfully clever and that sort of thing. There is nothing Lord Illingworth doesn't know.

LORD ILLINGWORTH

My dear boy!

GERALD

He knows more about life than any one I have ever met. I feel an awful duffer when I am with you, Lord Illingworth. Of course, I have had so few advantages. I have not been to Eton or Oxford like other chaps. But Lord Illingworth doesn't seem to mind that. He has been awfully good to me, mother.

MRS ARBUTHNOT

Lord Illingworth may change his mind. He may not really want you as his secretary.

GERALD

Mother!

MRS ARBUTHNOT

You must remember, as you said yourself, you have had so few advantages.

MRS ALLONBY

Lord Illingworth, I want to speak to you for a moment. Do come over.

him, Mrs Arbuthnot. Now that I have had the pleasure of meeting his mother I needn't say I appreciate him all the more. I think we are very alike in some things, Aleck and I.

Generally BLMS plays on the relationship between paternity, maternity and naming much more than the other drafts.

471 *know* LC, etc. (know. (*Puts his hand on* GERALD'S *shoulder*) Tiii, Tii, Ti).

472–85 *My dear boy . . . Do come over* (del. Tiii; om. LC).

475–6 *Eton or Oxford* the classic education for an aspiring civil servant, administrator, or politician in late nineteenth-century England was a major public school and then Oxford — particularly Balliol. (The influence of Balliol and its master, Jowett, on diplomatic life was enormous.)

477–8 *good to me, mother* BLMS adds 'no one has ever been so good to me, as he has.'

479 *Lord Illingworth may change his mind.* before this line Tii has an s.d. '(*Takes* GERALD *slightly L.C.*)'.

481 *Mother!* (Mother, why do you begin by making objections? C, BLi, BLMS; Mother, why do you say that? Tii).

482 *You must remember* C, BLi, BLMS add before this sentence: 'The objections may come ultimately from Lord Illingworth. I think they probably will.'

LORD ILLINGWORTH

Will you excuse me, Mrs Arbuthnot? Now, don't let your charming mother make any more difficulties, Gerald. The thing is quite settled, isn't it?

GERALD

I hope so.

LORD ILLINGWORTH *goes across to* MRS ALLONBY

MRS ALLONBY

I thought you were never going to leave the lady in black velvet.

LORD ILLINGWORTH

She is excessively handsome.

Looks at MRS ARBUTHNOT

LADY HUNSTANTON

Caroline, shall we all make a move to the music-room? Miss Worsley is going to play. You'll come too, dear Mrs Arbuthnot, won't you? You don't know what a treat is in store for you. (*To* DOCTOR DAUBENY) I must really take Miss Worsley down some afternoon to the rectory. I should so much like dear Mrs Daubeny to hear her on the violin. Ah, I forgot. Dear Mrs Daubeny's hearing is a little defective, is it not?

THE ARCHDEACON

Her deafness is a great privation to her. She can't even hear my sermons now. She reads them at home. But she has many resources in herself, many resources.

LADY HUNSTANTON

She reads a good deal, I suppose?

THE ARCHDEACON

Just the very largest print. The eyesight is rapidly going. But she's never morbid, never morbid.

GERALD (*To* LORD ILLINGWORTH)

Do speak to my mother, Lord Illingworth, before you go into the music-room. She seems to think, somehow, you don't mean what you said to me.

486 *Will you excuse me, Mrs Arbuthnot?* BLi (With pleasure. (*To* MRS ARBUTHNOT) Will you excuse me, Mrs Arbuthnot? Tiii, Tii, Ti, BLii). After the sentence Tii has an additional s.d.: '(*To* GERALD *arm on his shoulder*)'.

490 *I thought you were never going* before this sentence BLi, BLMS add: 'What is the extraordinary attraction that saints always have for sinners?'

492 s.d. see Appendix I.

501–11 *She can't even hear . . . In a few moments* (del. Ti; om. LC).

MRS ALLONBY
Aren't you coming?

LORD ILLINGWORTH
In a few moments. Lady Hunstanton, if Mrs Arbuthnot would allow me, I would like to say a few words to her, and we will join you later on.

LADY HUNSTANTON
Ah, of course. You will have a great deal to say to her, and she will have a great deal to thank you for. It is not every son who gets such an offer, Mrs Arbuthnot. But I know you appreciate that, dear.

LADY CAROLINE
John!

LADY HUNSTANTON
Now, don't keep Mrs Arbuthnot too long, Lord Illingworth. We can't spare her.

Exit following the other guests. Sound of violin heard from music-room

LORD ILLINGWORTH
So that is our son, Rachel! Well, I am very proud of him. He is a Harford, every inch of him. By the way, why Arbuthnot, Rachel?

MRS ARBUTHNOT
One name is as good as another, when one has no right to any name.

LORD ILLINGWORTH
I suppose so – But why Gerald?

MRS ARBUTHNOT
After a man whose heart I broke – after my father.

518 *John* Tiii Ti, BLii add the familiar joke here: 'SIR J: Yes, my love. (*Goes over to her*)'.
519–20 *Now don't . . . spare her* (del. Ti; om. LC). BLi and BLMS add here:
'And don't say any of your clever things to her. She doesn't know anything of the wickedness of this world, and mustn't be taught.'
520 s.d. Tiii has an additional direction in manuscript: '(LORD ILLINGWORTH *looks after* GERALD)'.
527 *after my father* BLi has an additional exchange following this line:
LORD I
And why Illingham of all places in the world?
MRS AR
I had hoped that in a little English village I would not meet anyone who had ever known me, but be alone with my child.

LORD ILLINGWORTH

Well, Rachel, what is over is over. All I have got to say now is that I am very, very much pleased with our boy. The world will know him merely as my private secretary, but to me he will be something very near, and very dear. It is a curious thing, Rachel; my life seemed to be quite complete. It was not so. It lacked something, it lacked a son. I have found my son now, I am glad I have found him.

MRS ARBUTHNOT

You have no right to claim him, or the smallest part of him. The boy is entirely mine, and shall remain mine.

LORD ILLINGWORTH

My dear Rachel, you have had him to yourself for over twenty years. Why not let me have him for a little now? He is quite as much mine as yours.

MRS ARBUTHNOT

Are you talking of the child you abandoned? Of the child who, as far as you are concerned, might have died of hunger and of want?

LORD ILLINGWORTH

You forget, Rachel, it was you who left me. It was not I who left you.

MRS ARBUTHNOT

I left you because you refused to give the child a name. Before my son was born, I implored you to marry me.

LORD ILLINGWORTH

I had no expectations then. And besides, Rachel, I wasn't much older than you were. I was only twenty-two. I was twenty-one, I believe, when the whole thing began in your father's garden.

531–4 *It is a . . . found him* LC, etc. (He is quite delightful C, BLi, BLMS).

538 *Why not let . . . little now* LC, etc. (It is only fair that I should have him now C, BLi, BLMS).

545 *refused to* C (would not LC, etc.).

546 *I implored you to marry me* (I implored you to marry me. You refused LC, Tiii, Ti, BLii, C; I implored you to marry me, not for my sake so much, but for his. You refused BLi, BLMS).

547 *I had no expectations then* LC, etc. (That was my mother's doing, Rachel. She knew all about the whole thing, of course, and she told me it would be perfect madness of me to think of marrying at my age. And it would have been. I had no expectations then. And what on earth would I have been doing with a wife all this time? BLi, BLMS).

549–50 *in your father's garden* (del. BLii; om. LC, Tiii, Ti).

MRS ARBUTHNOT
When a man is old enough to do wrong he should be old enough to do right also.

LORD ILLINGWORTH
My dear Rachel, intellectual generalities are always interesting, but generalities in morals mean absolutely nothing. As for saying I left our child to starve, that, of course, is untrue and silly. My mother offered you six hundred a year. But you wouldn't take anything. You simply disappeared, and carried the child away with you.

MRS ARBUTHNOT
I wouldn't have accepted a penny from her. Your father was different. He told you, in my presence, when we were in Paris, that it was your duty to marry me.

LORD ILLINGWORTH
Oh, duty is what one expects from others, it is not what one does oneself. Of course, I was influenced by my mother. Every man is when he is young.

MRS ARBUTHNOT
I am glad to hear you say so. Gerald shall certainly not go away with you.

LORD ILLINGWORTH
What nonsense, Rachel!

MRS ARBUTHNOT
Do you think I would allow my son –

LORD ILLINGWORTH
Our son.

553–4 *intellectual generalities . . . absolutely nothing* a familiar topic; Wilde incorporated this sentence into the early drafts of *Earnest*.
556 *six hundred a year* i.e. a very considerable sum. BLMS specifies £250, still a large sum, and adds: 'and you could have had any more you wanted merely by writing to her lawyer.'
559–60 *Your father was different* LC, etc. (Your father was different. He wanted you to marry me C, BLi, BLMS).
563 *does oneself* here C, BLi, BLMS add the following exchange:

MRS AR
Your father was an English gentleman.

LORD I
Yes, and my mother was an English lady. On my side Aleck has nothing to complain of his ancestry.

566 *with you* BLi and BLMS add to this sentence: 'His mother's influence will prevent him doing that.'

MRS ARBUTHNOT

My son (LORD ILLINGWORTH *shrugs his shoulders*) – to go away with the man who spoiled my youth, who ruined my life, who has tainted every moment of my days? You don't realise what my past has been in suffering and in shame.

LORD ILLINGWORTH

My dear Rachel, I must candidly say that I think Gerald's future considerably more important than your past.

MRS ARBUTHNOT

Gerald cannot separate his future from my past.

LORD ILLINGWORTH

That is exactly what he should do. That is exactly what you should help him to do. What a typical woman you are! You talk sentimentally, and you are thoroughly selfish the whole time. But don't let us have a scene. Rachel, I want you to look at this matter from the common-sense point of view, from the point of view of what is best for our son, leaving you and me out of the question. What is our son at present? An underpaid clerk in a small provincial bank in a third-rate English town. If you imagine he is quite happy in such a position, you are mistaken. He is thoroughly discontented.

MRS ARBUTHNOT

He was not discontented till he met you. You have made him so.

LORD ILLINGWORTH

Of course, I made him so. Discontent is the first step in the progress of a man or a nation. But I did not leave him with a mere longing for things he could not get. No, I made him

573 *my past ... and in shame* (it has cost me in suffering and in anguish to hide my secret BLi, BLMS; om. Tiii, Ti, LC).
574 *My dear Rachel* LC, etc. (My dear Rachel, what is the use of talking like that? C).
574 *I must ... that* (You must excuse me for saying so, but I confess LC, Tiii, Ti, BLii).
579–80 *whole time* C, BLi, BLMS add the following exchange:

MRS AR

No doubt if I were a man, I would be thoroughly selfish and talk with brutality.

LORD I

Well, we at any rate have the advantage of being candid.

580 *have a scene* LC, Tiii, Ti, BLii add: 'Scenes are for the middle-classes.'
581 *from the common-sense point of view* (om. LC).
581–4 *from the point ... third-rate English town* see Appendix I.
587–8 *have made him so* BLi, BLMS add: 'I saw something had changed him during the last few days.'
589–90 *first step ... or a nation* see Appendix I.

a charming offer. He jumped at it, I need hardly say. Any young man would. And now, simply because it turns out that I am the boy's own father and he my own son, you propose practically to ruin his career. That is to say, if I were a perfect stranger, you would allow Gerald to go away with me, but as he is my own flesh and blood you won't. How utterly illogical you are!

MRS ARBUTHNOT

I will not allow him to go.

LORD ILLINGWORTH

How can you prevent it? What excuse can you give to him for making him decline such an offer as mine? I won't tell him in what relations I stand to him, I need hardly say. But you daren't tell him. You know that. Look how you have brought him up.

MRS ARBUTHNOT

I have brought him up to be a good man.

LORD ILLINGWORTH

Quite so. And what is the result? You have educated him to be your judge if he ever finds you out. And a bitter, an unjust judge he will be to you. Don't be deceived, Rachel. Children

592–3 *Any young man would* C, BLi, BLMS add: 'His future was assured to him. I can do what I like in life.'

594 *he my own son* BLi, BLMS add: 'and there is a tie between us far nearer than that of mere friendship, or the interest of an elder in a younger man.' For the relationship between paternity and authority in the play, see Introduction.

597–8 *illogical you are* BLi, BLMS add: 'And in the whole matter you think entirely of yourself, you don't think of him.'

599 *I will not allow him to go* BLMS adds the following additional exchange:

LORD I

You absolutely refuse?

MRS AR

Yes.

LORD I

Because you have had what is called a painful past, you debar him from having a brilliant future. It comes to that?

MRS AR

I will not allow him to go.

603 *You know that* (Look how you have brought him up LC. You know that. And won't it be better, Rachel, that the boy should live away from you, seeing you of course from time to time when you want, should honour you, respect you, love you, as I know he does now, than that he should stay at home, and grow hard to you, be unkind to you, despise you. For he would despise you. Look how you have brought him up BLi, BLMS).

606 *Quite so* see Appendix I.

608–10 *Children begin . . . forgive them* another quotation taken virtually verbatim from *Dorian Gray*: 'Children begin by loving their parents; as they grow older they judge them; sometimes they forgive them.' (*DG*, p. 66/*CW*, p. 61.)

begin by loving their parents. After a time they judge them. Rarely, if ever, do they forgive them.

MRS ARBUTHNOT

George, don't take my son away from me. I have had twenty years of sorrow, and I have only had one thing to love me, only one thing to love. You have had a life of joy, and pleasure, and success. You have been quite happy, you have never thought of us. There was no reason, according to your views of life, why you should have remembered us at all. Your meeting us was a mere accident, a horrible accident. Forget it. Don't come now, and rob me of . . . of all I have, of all I have in the whole world. You are so rich in other things. Leave me the little vineyard of my life; leave me the walled-in garden and the well of water; the ewe-lamb God sent me, in pity or in wrath, oh! leave me that. George, don't take Gerald from me.

LORD ILLINGWORTH

Rachel, at the present moment you are not necessary to Gerald's career; I am. There is nothing more to be said on the subject.

MRS ARBUTHNOT

I will not let him go.

LORD ILLINGWORTH

Here is Gerald. He has a right to decide for himself.

Enter GERALD

GERALD

Well, dear mother, I hope you have settled it all with Lord Illingworth?

MRS ARBUTHNOT

I have not, Gerald.

LORD ILLINGWORTH

Your mother seems not to like your coming with me, for some reason.

GERALD

Why, mother?

624 *Rachel, at the present moment* BLi, BLMS (Rachel, you distress me by talking like that; and it is quite useless besides. At the present moment LC, Tiii, Ti, BLii).
628 *himself* BLi, BLMS add: 'I am quite ready to abide by his decision.'
634 *Why, mother?* BLi, BLMS add: 'You know I have set my heart on going.' At this point Tiii has a manuscript s.d. for Gerald: '*(Puts his arms around his mother's (?) neck)*'.

MRS ARBUTHNOT

I thought you were quite happy here with me, Gerald. I didn't know you were so anxious to leave me.

GERALD

Mother, how can you talk like that? Of course I have been quite happy with you. But a man can't stay always with his mother. No chap does. I want to make myself a position, to do something. I thought you would have been proud to see me Lord Illingworth's secretary.

MRS ARBUTHNOT

I do not think you would be suitable as a private secretary to Lord Illingworth. You have no qualifications.

LORD ILLINGWORTH

I don't wish to seem to interfere for a moment, Mrs Arbuthnot, but as far as your last objection is concerned, I surely am the best judge. And I can only tell you that your son has all the qualifications I had hoped for. He has more, in fact, than I had even thought of. Far more. (MRS ARBUTHNOT *remains silent*) Have you any other reason, Mrs Arbuthnot, why you don't wish your son to accept this post?

GERALD

Have you, mother? Do answer.

LORD ILLINGWORTH

If you have, Mrs Arbuthnot, pray, pray say it. We are quite by ourselves here. Whatever it is, I need not say I will not repeat it.

GERALD

Mother?

LORD ILLINGWORTH

If you would like to be alone with your son, I will leave you.

640 *do something* LC, etc. (do something, to go out in the world, to see the world. You seem to think that one has no ambition BLi, BLMS).

641 *Lord Illingworth's secretary* BLi, BLMS have the following additional exchange:

MRS AR

The world? The world? The less you see of the world, the better for you, Aleck.

ALECK

Mother, what can you know of the world? Nothing. Lord Illingworth knows the world better than you do, I need hardly say, and he finds it delightful. To run down the world is to run down life, as he says. The world is life. I want to live, mother.

650 *Mrs Arbuthnot* the Tiii typescript ends at this point.

You may have some other reason you don't wish me to hear.

MRS ARBUTHNOT

I have no other reason.

LORD ILLINGWORTH

Then, my dear boy, we may look on the thing as settled. Come, you and I will smoke a cigarette on the terrace together. And Mrs Arbuthnot, pray let me tell you, that I think you have acted very, very wisely.

Exit with GERALD. MRS ARBUTHNOT *is left alone. She stands immobile, with a look of unutterable sorrow on her face*

ACT DROP

Third Act

Scene – The Picture Gallery at Hunstanton. Door at back leading on to terrace.
LORD ILLINGWORTH *and* GERALD *R.C.* LORD ILLINGWORTH *lolling on a sofa.* GERALD *in a chair*

LORD ILLINGWORTH

Thoroughly sensible woman, your mother, Gerald. I knew she would come round in the end.

GERALD

My mother is awfully conscientious, Lord Illingworth, and I know she doesn't think I am educated enough to be your secretary. She is perfectly right, too. I was fearfully idle when I was at school, and I couldn't pass an examination now to save my life.

662 *terrace together* LC, etc. (terrace together and settle our plans for the future. A cigarette, as someone says, is the perfect type of the perfect pleasure. It is exquisite, and it leaves one unsatisfied. What more can one want? BLi, BLMS). The deleted quotation is of course from Wilde himself. (Cf. *DG*, p. 79/*CW*, p. 70.)

664 *very, very wisely* BLi, BLMS add the following:
'and that you will have no cause for regret that Aleck is coming with me.'

664 s.d. only in 1st ed.

LORD ILLINGWORTH

My dear Gerald, examinations are of no value whatsoever. If a man is a gentleman, he knows quite enough, and if he is not a gentleman, whatever he knows is bad for him.

GERALD

But I am so ignorant of the world, Lord Illingworth.

LORD ILLINGWORTH

Don't be afraid, Gerald. Remember that you've got on your side the most wonderful thing in the world – youth! There is nothing like youth. The middle-aged are mortgaged to Life. The old are in Life's lumber-room. But youth is the Lord of Life. Youth has a kingdom waiting for it. Every one is born a king, and most people die in exile, like most kings. To win back my youth, Gerald, there is nothing I wouldn't do – except take exercise, get up early, or be a useful member of the community.

GERALD

But you don't call yourself old, Lord Illingworth?

LORD ILLINGWORTH

I am old enough to be your father, Gerald.

GERALD

I don't remember my father; he died years ago.

LORD ILLINGWORTH

So Lady Hunstanton told me.

GERALD

It is very curious, my mother never talks to me about my

8 *My dear Gerald, examinations are of no value whatsoever* LC, etc. (Examinations are part of the serious twaddle of the nineteenth century. They are of no value whatsoever. C, BLMS). Cf. Lord Fermor in *Dorian Gray:* 'Examinations, sir, are pure humbug from beginning to end. If a man is a gentleman, he knows quite enough, and if he is not a gentleman, whatever he knows is bad for him'. (*DG*, p. 32/*CW*, p. 38.)

11–12 *But I am so ignorant ... Don't be afraid, Gerald* LC, etc. (But I am so ignorant of the world, Lord Illingworth, and I'm afraid to appear in it.

LORD I:

You could never be awkward, Aleck. You are much too delightful. A certain amount of shyness is rather attractive to women, if one cares to keep it up. But it is a trouble in the end. People get to think that one is absolutely harmless and that is an inconvenient reputation to have C, BLMS).

18 *nothing I wouldn't do* LC, etc. (I would do anything in the world C, BLMS.) Lord I's speech borrows directly from Lord Henry Wotton in *Dorian Gray:* 'To get back my youth I would do anything in the world, except take exercise, get up early, or be respectable. Youth! There is nothing like it.' (*DG*, p. 216/*CW*, p. 162.)

father. I sometimes think she must have married beneath her.

LORD ILLINGWORTH (*Winces slightly*)
Really? (*Goes over and puts his hand on* GERALD*'s shoulder*) You have missed not having a father, I suppose, Gerald?

GERALD
Oh, no; my mother has been so good to me. No one ever had such a mother as I have had.

LORD ILLINGWORTH
I am quite sure of that. Still I should imagine that most mothers don't quite understand their sons. Don't realise, I mean, that a son has ambitions, a desire to see life, to make himself a name. After all, Gerald, you couldn't be expected to pass all your life in such a hole as Wrockley, could you?

GERALD
Oh, no! It would be dreadful!

LORD ILLINGWORTH
A mother's love is very touching, of course, but it is often curiously selfish. I mean, there is a good deal of selfishness in it.

GERALD (*Slowly*)
I suppose there is.

LORD ILLINGWORTH
Your mother is a thoroughly good woman. But good women have such limited views of life, their horizon is so small, their interests are so petty, aren't they?

GERALD
They are awfully interested, certainly, in things we don't care much about.

LORD ILLINGWORTH
I suppose your mother is very religious, and that sort of thing.

26–9 *I sometimes think . . . I suppose, Gerald* LC, etc. (I sometimes fancy that they were not happy together. Or perhaps they were so happy that it would give her pain to talk of him. LORD I: I should imagine that was the reason. Your mother is such a charming woman. You have missed not having a father, Aleck. You have a little, I suppose? BLMS).

34–5 *make himself a name* BLMS adds here: 'Your mother is the most admirable woman in the world, I have no doubt, and I quite understand how fond she is of you, but I must say it struck me in the conversation I had with her alone, and when we three were together, that she thought [a] little too much of herself, at any rate, didn't think enough of you.'

36 *Wrockley* LC, etc. (Allingham BLMS). Neither place exists.

GERALD

Oh, yes, she's always going to church.

LORD ILLINGWORTH

Ah! she is not modern, and to be modern is the only thing worth being nowadays. You want to be modern, don't you, Gerald? You want to know life as it really is. Not to be put off with any old-fashioned theories about life. Well, what you have to do at present is simply to fit yourself for the best society. A man who can dominate a London dinner-table can dominate the world. The future belongs to the dandy. It is the exquisites who are going to rule.

GERALD

I should like to wear nice things awfully, but I have always been told that a man should not think too much about his clothes.

LORD ILLINGWORTH

People nowadays are so absolutely superficial that they don't understand the philosophy of the superficial. By the way, Gerald, you should learn how to tie your tie better. Sentiment is all very well for the button-hole. But the essential thing for a necktie is style. A well-tied tie is the first serious step in life.

GERALD (*Laughing*)

I might be able to learn how to tie a tie, Lord Illingworth, but I should never be able to talk as you do. I don't know how to talk.

49–57 *Oh, yes, she's always ... going to rule* see Appendix I.

56 *The future belongs to the dandy* the supremacy of style is another central Wildean theme. Cf. 'A Few Maxims for the Instruction of the Over-Educated': 'Dandyism is the assertion of the absolute modernity of Beauty' (*CW*, p. 1204) and Gwendolen in *Earnest* (III, 28–9): 'In matters of grave importance, style, not sincerity is the vital thing.' (*CW*, p. 371.)

58–9 *I have always been told* (my mother says LC, etc).

61–2 *People are so absolutely ... philosophy of the superficial* LC, etc. (Oh, women are so tedious about that sort of thing. They are so absolutely superficial themselves, that they don't understand the philosophy of the superficial C, BLMS).

62–6 *By the way ... step in life* LC, etc. Before this sentence, T, BLii, BLi have the following: 'They can't realise that in the mere knotting of a necktie or the choice of a buttonhole, there is a whole creed of life. In point of fact, women like us badly dressed. They are a little afraid of the dandy. They want appearances to be against us — appearances usually are.' C is similar.

The sentiment is familiar: it appears in other plays, *Dorian Gray*, and in *Husband*, I, 21 s.d. where the Vicomte de Nanjac is 'known for his neckties and his Anglomania'.

67 *I might be ... Lord Illingworth* LC, etc. (It would be delightful to be what you call a dandy BLMS).

LORD ILLINGWORTH

Oh! talk to every woman as if you loved her, and to every man as if he bored you, and at the end of your first season you will have the reputation of possessing the most perfect social tact.

GERALD

But it is very difficult to get into society, isn't it?

LORD ILLINGWORTH

To get into the best society, nowadays, one has either to feed people, amuse people, or shock people – that is all.

GERALD

I suppose society is wonderfully delightful!

LORD ILLINGWORTH

To be in it is merely a bore. But to be out of it simply a tragedy. Society is a necessary thing. No man has any real success in this world unless he has got women to back him, and women rule society. If you have not got women on your side you are quite over. You might just as well be a barrister, or a stockbroker, or a journalist at once.

GERALD

It is very difficult to understand women, is it not?

LORD ILLINGWORTH

You should never try to understand them. Women are pictures. Men are problems. If you want to know what a woman really means – which, by the way, is always a dangerous thing to do – look at her, don't listen to her.

GERALD

But women are awfully clever, aren't they?

LORD ILLINGWORTH

One should always tell them so. But, to the philosopher, my dear Gerald, women represent the triumph of matter over

72–3 *possessing the most perfect social tact* (being a young man of perfect social tact LC etc.). Following this line, LC, BLii, BLi have an additional s.d.:

Servants bring on a tray with lemonade, etc., on it and place it on table R.C.

82 *barrister* C, BLi (lawyer LC, etc.).

83 *stockbroker* another familiar butt for Wilde's humour. Cf. *Earnest*: 'It is very vulgar to talk about one's business. Only people like stockbrokers do that, and then merely at dinner parties.' (*Earnest*, II, 824–6/*CW*, p. 368.)

90 *to the philosopher* LC etc. (as a mere matter of fact C, BLMS). Lord Illingworth's speech is taken virtually verbatim from *Dorian Gray*: 'Women represent the triumph of matter over mind, just as men represent the triumph of mind over morals.' (*DG*, p. 47/*CW*, p. 48.)

mind – just as men represent the triumph of mind over morals.

GERALD

How then can women have so much power as you say they have?

LORD ILLINGWORTH

The history of women is the history of the worst form of tyranny the world has ever known. The tyranny of the weak over the strong. It is the only tyranny that lasts.

GERALD

But haven't women got a refining influence?

LORD ILLINGWORTH

Nothing refines but the intellect.

GERALD

Still, there are many different kinds of women, aren't there?

LORD ILLINGWORTH

Only two kinds in society: the plain and the coloured.

GERALD

But there are good women in society, aren't there?

LORD ILLINGWORTH

Far too many.

GERALD

But do you think women shouldn't be good?

LORD ILLINGWORTH

One should never tell them so, they'd all become good at once. Women are a fascinatingly wilful sex. Every woman is a rebel, and usually in wild revolt against herself.

GERALD

You have never been married, Lord Illingworth, have you?

97–8 *weak over the strong* BLii, etc. (charming over the tedious LC, T).

103 *the plain and the coloured* a metaphor taken from nineteenth-century toy theatre sheets — the plain cost one penny, the coloured twopence. Cf. also *Dorian Gray*: 'I find that, ultimately, that there are only two kinds of women, the plain and the coloured.' (*DG*, p. 47/*CW*, p. 48.)

105 *Far too many* see Appendix I.

109 *revolt against herself* LC, T add a s.d. here: '(*Sits down again*).'

110 *You have never been married, Lord Illingworth, have you*? LC, etc. (You have never been married, Lord Illingworth, have you? LORD I: No. GERALD: I wonder why. BLi).

LORD ILLINGWORTH
Men marry because they are tired; women because they are curious. Both are disappointed.

GERALD
But don't you think one can be happy when one is married?

LORD ILLINGWORTH
Perfectly happy. But the happiness of a married man, my dear Gerald, depends on the people he has not married.

GERALD
But if one is in love?

LORD ILLINGWORTH
One should always be in love. That is the reason one should never marry.

GERALD
Love is a very wonderful thing, isn't it?

LORD ILLINGWORTH
When one is in love one begins by deceiving oneself. And one ends by deceiving others. That is what the world calls a romance. But a really *grande passion* is comparatively rare nowadays. It is the privilege of people who have nothing to do. That is the one use of the idle classes in a country, and the only possible explanation of us Harfords.

GERALD
Harfords, Lord Illingworth?

LORD ILLINGWORTH
That is my family name. You should study the Peerage, Gerald. It is the one book a young man about town should

111–2 *Men marry . . . Both are disappointed* another borrowing from *Dorian Gray*: 'Men marry because they are tired; women, because they are curious; both are disappointed.' (*DG*, p. 46/*CW*, p. 48.)

120–3 *When one is in love . . . nowadays* T, etc. (om. LC). The idea of the necessity of deceit is a theme common in Wilde. It is central to *Lady Windermere's Fan*. Cf. also *Dorian Gray*: 'When one is in love, one always begins by deceiving oneself, and one always ends by deceiving others. That is what the world calls a romance.' (*DG*, p. 52/*CW*, p. 52.)

120–33 *When one is in love . . . should live in it*! see Appendix I.

123–4 *It is the privilege . . . in a country* another borrowing from *Dorian Gray*: 'A *grande passion* is the privilege of people who have nothing to do. That is the one use of the idle classes of a country.' (*DG*, p. 48/*CW*, pp. 49-50.)

127 *Peerage* a possible reference is to *Burke's Peerage, Baronetage and Knightage* which appeared first in 1826. However Burke only lists extant peers and so a more likely reference is to G.E. Cokayne's *Complete Peerage* (1884–98), the publication of which coincided with Wilde's career.

know thoroughly, and it is the best thing in fiction the English have ever done. And now, Gerald, you are going now into a perfectly new life with me, and I want you to know how to live. (MRS ARBUTHNOT *appears on terrace behind*) For the world has been made by fools that wise men should live in it!

Enter L.C. LADY HUNSTANTON *and* DR DAUBENY

LADY HUNSTANTON
Ah! here you are, dear Lord Illingworth. Well, I suppose you have been telling our young friend, Gerald, what his new duties are to be, and giving him a great deal of good advice over a pleasant cigarette.

LORD ILLINGWORTH
I have been giving him the best of advice, Lady Hunstanton, and the best of cigarettes.

LADY HUNSTANTON
I am so sorry I was not here to listen to you, but I suppose I am too old now to learn. Except from you, dear Archdeacon, when you are in your nice pulpit. But then I always know what you are going to say, so I don't feel alarmed. (*Sees* MRS ARBUTHNOT) Ah! dear Mrs Arbuthnot, do come and join us. Come, dear. (*Enter* MRS ARBUTHNOT) Gerald has been having such a long talk with Lord Illingworth; I am sure you must feel very much flattered at the pleasant way in which everything has turned out for him. Let us sit down. (*They sit down*) And how is your beautiful embroidery going on?

MRS ARBUTHNOT
I am always at work, Lady Hunstanton.

LADY HUNSTANTON
Mrs Daubeny embroiders a little, too, doesn't she?

THE ARCHDEACON
She was very deft with her needle once, quite a Dorcas. But the gout has crippled her fingers a good deal. She has not

133 s.d. It appears to have been Wilde's original intention to include extra material at this point in the act, for he instructed his typist in BLMS to leave a blank page. The blank page was retained through BLi and C.

134 *dear Lord Illingworth* BLMS adds here: 'Everyone has been looking for you. (*To* DR DAUBENY) Except poor Lady Caroline, who has been looking for Sir John. Spoiling him as usual.'

139 *and the best of cigarettes* (I have explained to him that duties are a thing of the past BLi, C, BLMS; om. C).

148 *Let us sit down.* (They sit down) BLii, etc. (om. LC).

152 *Dorcas* 'name of a woman mentioned in Acts ix. 36; hence, *Dorcas Society*, a ladies' association in a church for making and providing clothes for the poor' (*OED*).

touched the tambour frame for nine or ten years. But she has many other amusements. She is very much interested in her own health.

LADY HUNSTANTON
Ah! that is always a nice distraction, is it not? Now, what are you talking about, Lord Illingworth? Do tell us.

LORD ILLINGWORTH
I was on the point of explaining to Gerald that the world has always laughed at its own tragedies, that being the only way in which it has been able to bear them. And that, consequently, whatever the world has treated seriously belongs to the comedy side of things.

LADY HUNSTANTON
Now I am quite out of my depth. I usually am when Lord Illingworth says anything. And the Humane Society is most careless. They never rescue me. I am left to sink. I have a dim idea, dear Lord Illingworth, that you are always on the side of the sinners, and I know I always try to be on the side of the saints, but that is as far as I get. And after all, it may be merely the fancy of a drowning person.

LORD ILLINGWORTH
The only difference between the saint and the sinner is that every saint has a past, and every sinner has a future.

LADY HUNSTANTON
Ah! that quite does for me. I haven't a word to say. You and I, dear Mrs Arbuthnot, are behind the age. We can't follow Lord Illingworth. Too much care was taken with our education, I am afraid. To have been well brought up is a great drawback nowadays. It shuts one out from so much.

MRS ARBUTHNOT
I should be sorry to follow Lord Illingworth in any of his opinions.

154 *tambour frame* 'a circular frame formed of one hoop fitting within another, in which silk, muslin, or other material is stretched for embroidering' (*OED*).

157 *is it not?* at this point the early drafts have an additional speech for Gerald: 'Oh, I would like to see India!' The line underwent revision in T, BLii, C and was omitted from LC.

157–8 *Now, what are you talking about, Lord Illingworth?* LC, etc. (Now, what are you talking about, Lord Illingworth? I am sure it is something very interesting. BLMS).

165–6 *And the Humane Society . . . left to sink* (del. T; om. LC). The Humane Society was a society for the rescue of drowning persons. It was founded as the Royal Humane Society in 1774.

169–70 *And after all . . . a drowning person* (del. T; om. LC).

176–7 *To have been . . . from so much* (del. T; om. LC).

LADY HUNSTANTON
You are quite right, dear.

GERALD *shrugs his shoulders and looks irritably over at his mother. Enter* LADY CAROLINE

LADY CAROLINE
Jane, have you seen John anywhere?

LADY HUNSTANTON
You needn't be anxious about him, dear. He is with Lady Stutfield; I saw them some time ago, in the Yellow Drawing-room. They seem quite happy together. You are not going, Caroline? Pray sit down.

LADY CAROLINE
I think I had better look after John. *Exit* LADY CAROLINE

LADY HUNSTANTON
It doesn't do to pay men so much attention. And Caroline has really nothing to be anxious about. Lady Stutfield is very sympathetic. She is just as sympathetic about one thing as she is about another. A beautiful nature.

Enter SIR JOHN *and* MRS ALLONBY

Ah! here is Sir John! And with Mrs Allonby too! I suppose it was Mrs Allonby I saw him with. Sir John, Caroline has been looking everywhere for you.

MRS ALLONBY
We have been waiting for her in the Music-room, dear Lady Hunstanton.

LADY HUNSTANTON
Ah! the Music-room, of course. I thought it was the Yellow Drawing-room, my memory is getting so defective. (*To the* ARCHDEACON) Mrs Daubeny has a wonderful memory, hasn't she?

180 s.d. BLMS has an additional speech for Lord I to cover Lady C's entrance:
'LORD I:
Your mother means well, my dear boy. But she has lived very little in the world. Don't mind her.'

186 s.d. in BLMS Lady C's exit is delayed until the third sentence of Lady H's speech, which there begins: 'You spoil him, Caroline. I have often told you so.' In LC, T, BLii, BLi Lady C exits immediately following her last speech and Lady H's opening sentences are changed to: 'She spoils him, dear Rector, she spoils him.'

190 *a beautiful nature* here BLMS adds the following exchange:
LORD I
Comédienne avec trop de coeur. That is what Lady Stutfield is. I delight in her.
LADY H
You wretch, you delight in everyone who is pretty. And quite right, too.

THE ARCHDEACON

She used to be quite remarkable for her memory, but since her last attack she recalls chiefly the events of her early childhood. But she finds great pleasure in such retrospections, great pleasure.

Enter LADY STUTFIELD *and* MR KELVIL

LADY HUNSTANTON

Ah! dear Lady Stutfield! and what has Mr Kelvil been talking to you about?

LADY STUTFIELD

About Bimetallism, as well as I remember.

LADY HUNSTANTON

Bimetallism! Is that quite a nice subject? However, I know people discuss everything very freely nowadays. What did Sir John talk to you about, dear Mrs Allonby?

MRS ALLONBY

About Patagonia.

LADY HUNSTANTON

Really? What a remote topic! But very improving, I have no doubt.

MRS ALLONBY

He has been most interesting on the subject of Patagonia. Savages seem to have quite the same views as cultured people on almost all subjects. They are excessively advanced.

LADY HUNSTANTON

What do they do?

MRS ALLONBY

Apparently everything.

204–13 *Ah! dear Lady Stutfield . . . subject of Patagonia* see Appendix I.

206 *Bimetallism* 'The system of allowing the unrestricted currency of two metals (e.g. gold and silver) at a fixed ratio to each other, as coined money' (*OED*). In *Earnest* Cecily is studying political economy under Miss Prism's tutelage (II, 1–93). Cf. also *Husband*, II, 453. In 1893 John Walter Cross, the husband and biographer of George Eliot, published *Impressions of Dante and of The New World, with a Few Words on Bimetallism*. The absurdity of the title would not have been lost on Wilde.

210 *Patagonia* i.e. a region of Chile and Argentina in South America. It was the subject of much scientific exploration in the late nineteenth century. The Patagonians were reputed to be physically immense: hence the place implied remoteness or strangeness.

217 *Apparently everything* at this point LC, T, BLii have an entrance for Lord A and Lady S.

LADY HUNSTANTON
Well, it is very gratifying, dear Archdeacon, is it not, to find that Human Nature is permanently one. – On the whole, the world is the same world, is it not?

LORD ILLINGWORTH
The world is simply divided into two classes – those who believe the incredible, like the public – and those who do the improbable –

MRS ALLONBY
Like yourself?

LORD ILLINGWORTH
Yes; I am always astonishing myself. It is the only thing that makes life worth living.

LADY STUTFIELD
And what have you been doing lately that astonishes you?

LORD ILLINGWORTH
I have been discovering all kinds of beautiful qualities in my own nature.

MRS ALLONBY
Ah! don't become quite perfect all at once. Do it gradually!

LORD ILLINGWORTH
I don't intend to grow perfect at all. At least, I hope I shan't. It would be most inconvenient. Women love us for our defects. If we have enough of them, they will forgive us everything, even our gigantic intellects.

MRS ALLONBY
It is premature to ask us to forgive analysis. We forgive adoration; that is quite as much as should be expected from us.

219 *Human Nature is permanently one* LC, etc. (Human Nature is permanently one. Of course colour and clothes make a great difference no doubt. So many of the duskier nations have so much of the one and so little of the other BLMS).

221–3 *those who believe the incredible ... do the improbable* another sentiment from *Dorian Gray*: 'Henry spends his days in saying what is incredible and his evenings in doing what is improbable.' (*DG*, p. 116/*CW*, p. 95.)

232–5 *It would be ... forgive analysis* (del. T; om. LC).

232–3 *Women love us for our defects* (My experience is women love us for our defects T, BLii, BLi). The sentiment is taken directly from *Dorian Gray*: 'Women love us for our defects. If we have enough of them they will forgive us everything, even our intellects.' (*DG*, p. 179/*CW*, p. 137.) Cf. Mabel Chiltern in *Husband* who 'delights in' Lord Goring's 'bad qualities' (I, 224–31).

235–7 *We forgive adoration ... expected from us* (del. T; om. LC). T, BLii have an additional speech for Lady S: 'Yes, quite, quite as much.'

Enter LORD ALFRED. *He joins* LADY STUTFIELD

LADY HUNSTANTON
Ah! we women should forgive everything, shouldn't we, dear Mrs Arbuthnot? I am sure you agree with me in that.

MRS ARBUTHNOT
I do not, Lady Hunstanton. I think there are many things women should never forgive.

LADY HUNSTANTON
What sort of things?

MRS ARBUTHNOT
The ruin of another woman's life.

Moves slowly away to back of stage

LADY HUNSTANTON
Ah! those things are very sad, no doubt, but I believe there are admirable homes where people of that kind are looked after and reformed, and I think on the whole that the secret of life is to take things very, very easily.

MRS ALLONBY
The secret of life is never to have an emotion that is unbecoming.

LADY STUTFIELD
The secret of life is to appreciate the pleasure of being terribly, terribly deceived.

KELVIL
The secret of life is to resist temptation, Lady Stutfield.

LORD ILLINGWORTH
There is no secret of life. Life's aim, if it has one, is simply

237 s.d. in BLMS Sir John enters instead of Lord A; in C Mr K enters.
238 *Ah! we women should forgive everything* LC, etc. (Ah! we women should forgive everything. Dear Lady Stutfield! Do find a comfortable seat. Yes: we should forgive everything BLMS).
243 s.d. (om. LC, etc.).
245 *admirable homes* 'rescue' homes, whose purpose was the rehabilitation of fallen women and prostitutes, were one of the commonest forms of contemporary philanthropy. Lady H's reference is to an institution like the Female Middle Class Emigration Society (which operated from 1862 to 1886). The London Rescue Society attempted to help fallen women from the lower and working classes. Other institutions to redeem prostitutes were the House of Refuge, Redemption Societies and various forms of assisted emigration.
252 *The secret of life is to resist temptation, Lady Stutfield* in T, BLii C, BLi, BLMS this speech is given to Mrs Ar. Absence of self-control is a theme common to Wilde's oeuvre. Cf. Lord Darlington in *LWF*: 'I couldn't help it. I can resist everything except temptation.' (*LWF* I, 139–40/*CW*, p. 388.)

to be always looking for temptations. There are not nearly enough. I sometimes pass a whole day without coming across a single one. It is quite dreadful. It makes one so nervous about the future.

LADY HUNSTANTON (*Shakes her fan at him*)
I don't know how it is, dear Lord Illingworth, but everything you have said today seems to me excessively immoral. It has been most interesting, listening to you.

LORD ILLINGWORTH
All thought is immoral. Its very essence is destruction. If you think of anything, you kill it. Nothing survives being thought of.

LADY HUNSTANTON
I don't understand a word, Lord Illingworth. But I have no doubt it is all quite true. Personally, I have very little to reproach myself with, on the score of thinking. I don't believe in women thinking too much. Women should think in moderation, as they should do all things in moderation.

LORD ILLINGWORTH
Moderation is a fatal thing, Lady Hunstanton. Nothing succeeds like excess.

LADY HUNSTANTON
I hope I shall remember that. It sounds an admirable maxim. But I'm beginning to forget everything. It's a great misfortune.

LORD ILLINGWORTH
It is one of your most fascinating qualities, Lady Hunstanton. No women should have a memory. Memory in a woman is the beginning of dowdiness. One can always tell from a woman's bonnet whether she has got a memory or not.

LADY HUNSTANTON
How charming you are, dear Lord Illingworth. You always find out that one's most glaring fault is one's most important virtue. You have the most comforting views of life.

269–70 *Nothing succeeds like excess* (Enough is as bad as a meal, more than enough is as good as a feast. Nothing succeeds like excess LC, T, BLii, C, BLi; Enough is as bad as a meal, more than enough is as good as a feast BLMS).

274 *your most fascinating qualities, Lady Hunstanton* C, BLMS add here: 'There is something perfectly awful about the memories of most women — they are always exhuming the past, and bothering one about the things one has said or done as if it was any matter what one has said or done.'

280 *You have the most comforting views of life* (del. T; om. LC).

Enter FARQUHAR

FARQUHAR
Doctor Daubeny's carriage!

LADY HUNSTANTON
My dear Archdeacon! It is only half-past ten.

THE ARCHDEACON (*Rising*)
I am afraid I must go, Lady Hunstanton. Tuesday is always one of Mrs Daubeny's bad nights.

LADY HUNSTANTON (*Rising*)
Well, I won't keep you from her. (*Goes with him towards door*) I have told Farquhar to put a brace of partridge into the carriage. Mrs Daubeny may fancy them.

THE ARCHDEACON
It is very kind of you, but Mrs Daubeny never touches solids now. Lives entirely on jellies. But she is wonderfully cheerful, wonderfully cheerful. She has nothing to complain of.

Exit with LADY HUNSTANTON

MRS ALLONBY (*Goes over to* LORD ILLINGWORTH)
There is a beautiful moon tonight.

LORD ILLINGWORTH
Let us go and look at it. To look at anything that is inconstant is charming nowadays.

MRS ALLONBY
You have your looking-glass.

LORD ILLINGWORTH
It is unkind. It merely shows me my wrinkles.

MRS ALLONBY
Mine is better behaved. It never tells me the truth.

LORD ILLINGWORTH
Then it is in love with you.

285 *keep you from her* here BLMS adds: '(DOCTOR DAUBENY *offers to shake hands*.) Oh! I'll see you as far as the Hall, Rector. We're old enough friends for that.'
In LC, T, BLii, BLi Dr D has a separate speech to cover his exit:
DR D (*To company*)
Goodnight! Goodnight! (*To* MRS ARBUTHNOT)
Goodnight, Mrs Arbuthnot!

290 s.d. ([*Exit with* LADY HUNSTANTON. SIR JOHN *and* LADY STUTFIELD *follow*.] BLMS).

295 *It is unkind* LC, etc. (It is unkind. It shows me none of my nice qualities. BLMS).

Exeunt SIR JOHN, LADY STUTFIELD, MR KELVIL, *and* LORD ALFRED

GERALD (*To* LORD ILLINGWORTH)
May I come too?

LORD ILLINGWORTH
Do, my dear boy.

Moves towards door with MRS ALLONBY *and* GERALD

LADY CAROLINE *enters, looks rapidly round, and goes out in opposite direction to that taken by* SIR JOHN *and* LADY STUTFIELD

MRS ARBUTHNOT
Gerald!

GERALD
What, mother!

Exit LORD ILLINGWORTH *with* MRS ALLONBY

MRS ARBUTHNOT
It is getting late. Let us go home.

GERALD
My dear mother. Do let us wait a little longer. Lord Illingworth is so delightful, and, by the way, mother, I have a great surprise for you. We are starting for India at the end of this month.

MRS ARBUTHNOT
Let us go home.

GERALD
If you really want to, of course, mother, but I must bid good-bye to Lord Illingworth first. I'll be back in five minutes. *Exit*

MRS ARBUTHNOT
Let him leave me if he chooses, but not with him – not with him! I couldn't bear it. *Walks up and down*

Enter HESTER

297 s.d. (om. BLMS). In LC and C Mr K has no exit here; in BLi Mrs Al exits instead of him.
298–9 *May I come . . . my dear boy* (del. T; om. LC).
300–3 *Gerald! . . . a little longer* (del. T; om. LC).
303 *My dear mother*. T, etc. (My dear mother. It is quite early. BLMS).
303–12 *Lord Illingworth is . . . not with him* (del. T; om. LC).
306 *end of this month* BLMS adds here: 'We are going round the world. Isn't it charming?' (Perhaps the tone of this is too like Lord Illingworth's and hence its deletion.)

HESTER

What a lovely night it is, Mrs Arbuthnot.

MRS ARBUTHNOT

Is it?

HESTER

Mrs Arbuthnot, I wish you would let us be friends. You are so different from the other women here. When you came into the drawing-room this evening, somehow you brought with you a sense of what is good and pure in life. I had been foolish. There are things that are right to say, but that may be said at the wrong time and to the wrong people.

MRS ARBUTHNOT

I heard what you said. I agree with it, Miss Worsley.

HESTER

I didn't know you had heard it. But I knew you would agree with me. A woman who has sinned should be punished, shouldn't she?

MRS ARBUTHNOT

Yes.

HESTER

She shouldn't be allowed to come into the society of good men and women?

MRS ARBUTHNOT

She should not.

HESTER

And the man should be punished in the same way?

MRS ARBUTHNOT

In the same way. And the children, if there are children, in the same way also?

HESTER

Yes, it is right that the sins of the parents should be visited on the children. It is a just law. It is God's law.

314 *Is it?* LC, etc. (Is it? I have not noticed it, Miss Worsley. C, BLMS).
315 *I wish you would let us be friends* LC, etc, (I wish you would let me know you better. Your son has spoken to me so much about you, I seem to know you quite well C, BLMS).
332 *sins of the parents* the reference is to the Commandments. See *Exodus* 20.5; 'I am the Lord thy God, mighty, jealous, visiting the iniquity of the fathers upon the children, unto the third and fourth generation of them that hate me.'
333 *It is God's law* see Appendix I.

MRS ARBUTHNOT
It is one of God's terrible laws.

Moves away to fireplace

HESTER
You are distressed about your son leaving you, Mrs Arbuthnot?

MRS ARBUTHNOT
Yes.

HESTER
Do you like him going away with Lord Illingworth? Of course there is position, no doubt, and money, but position and money are not everything, are they?

MRS ARBUTHNOT
They are nothing; they bring misery.

HESTER
Then why do you let your son go with him?

MRS ARBUTHNOT
He wishes it himself.

HESTER
But if you asked him he would stay, would he not?

MRS ARBUTHNOT
He has set his heart on going.

HESTER
He couldn't refuse you anything. He loves you too much. Ask him to stay. Let me send him in to you. He is on the terrace at this moment with Lord Illingworth. I heard them laughing together as I passed through the Music-room.

334 s.d. ([*Looks away and wipes her eyes with her handkerchief*] LC, T, BLi; om. BLMS).

335–7 *You are distressed. . . . Yes* LC, etc. (You are distressed about your son leaving you, Mrs Arbuthnot. I know you will miss him very much.
MRS AR:
Yes. I will miss him very much. BLMS).

338 *going away with Lord Illingworth?* see Appendix I.

346–7 *Ask him to stay* BLMS adds here: 'I think it is your duty. You don't know Lord Illingworth well enough yet, do you? You don't know what his life has been or may be.'

348–9 *I heard them . . . Music-room* BLi, etc. (om. LC, T, BLii).

MRS ARBUTHNOT

Don't trouble, Miss Worsley, I can wait. It is of no consequence.

HESTER

No, I'll tell him you want him. Do – do ask him to stay.

Exit HESTER

MRS ARBUTHNOT

He won't come – I know he won't come.

Enter LADY CAROLINE. *She looks round anxiously*

Enter GERALD

LADY CAROLINE

Mr Arbuthnot, may I ask you is Sir John anywhere on the terrace?

GERALD

No, Lady Caroline, he is not on the terrace.

LADY CAROLINE

It is very curious. It is time for him to retire.

Exit LADY CAROLINE

GERALD

Dear mother, I am afraid I kept you waiting. I forgot all about it. I am so happy tonight, mother; I have never been so happy.

MRS ARBUTHNOT

At the prospect of going away?

350 *Don't trouble, Miss Worsley, I can wait* LC, etc. (Don't trouble, I am waiting for him here. We are going home at once. I am afraid he has forgotten about it.

MABEL.

I'll send him in to you.

MRS AR

I can wait BLMS).

353 *He won't come — I know he won't come* ([*Wipes her eyes with her handkerchief*] He won't come — I know he won't come LC, T, BLii, BLi; I mustn't let him see I have been crying. [*Wipes her eyes with her handkerchief*] Why are we women made to cry? That men may weary of us, I suppose BLMS; I mustn't let him see I've been crying. [*Wipes her eyes with her handkerchief*] Why are we women made to cry? C).

353 s.d. T, BLii, BLi cover the entrance of Gerald and Lady C with the following exchange:

LADY C

Sir John is not here, Mrs Arbuthnot, is he?

MRS AR

No, Lady Caroline.

In LC Lady C has no entrance (nor subsequent exit). In this text Gerald has an entrance at this point, although he has had no previous exit.

358–9 *I forgot all about it* (om. T, LC).

361 *At the prospect of going away* LC, etc. (At the prospect of going away from Allingham BLMS).

GERALD

Don't put it like that, mother. Of course I am sorry to leave you. Why, you are the best mother in the whole world. But after all, as Lord Illingworth says, it is impossible to live in such a place as Wrockley. You don't mind it. But I'm ambitious; I want something more than that. I want to have a career. I want to do something that will make you proud of me, and Lord Illingworth is going to help me. He is going to do everything for me.

MRS ARBUTHNOT

Gerald, don't go away with Lord Illingworth. I implore you not to. Gerald, I beg you!

GERALD

Mother, how changeable you are! You don't seem to know your own mind for a single moment. An hour and a half ago in the drawing-room you agreed to the whole thing; now you turn round and make objections, and try to force me to give up my one chance in life. Yes, my one chance. You don't suppose that men like Lord Illingworth are to be found every day, do you, mother? It is very strange that when I have had such a wonderful piece of good luck, the one person to put difficulties in my way should be my own mother. Besides, you know, mother, I love Hester Worsley. Who could help loving her? I love her more than I have ever told you, far more. And if I had a position, if I had prospects, I could – I could ask her to – Don't you understand now, mother, what it means to me to be Lord Illingworth's secretary? To start like that is to find a career ready for one – before one – waiting for one. If I were Lord Illingworth's secretary I could ask Hester to be my wife. As a wretched bank clerk with a hundred a year it would be an impertinence.

MRS ARBUTHNOT

I fear you need have no hopes of Miss Worsley. I know her views on life. She has just told them to me.

A pause

363 *best mother in the whole world* BLMS adds here: 'You know I love you, mother, don't you?'
365 *Wrockley* LC, etc. (Allingham C, BLMS).
365–9 *But I'm ambitious . . . everything for me* see Appendix I.
370–1 *I implore you not to. Gerald, I beg you!* (del. T; om. LC).
377–8 *found every day, do you, mother* BLMS adds here: 'or that such a post as he offers is to be got simply for the asking?'
382 *I have ever told you, far more* LC, etc. (I have ever told you, more than I can ever tell her BLMS).
383 *if I had prospects* LC, etc. (If I had prospects, if I had a career before me BLMS).

GERALD

Then I have my ambition left, at any rate. That is something – I am glad I have that! You have always tried to crush my ambition, mother – haven't you? You have told me that the world is a wicked place, that success is not worth having, that society is shallow, and all that sort of thing – well, I don't believe it, mother. I think the world must be delightful. I think society must be exquisite. I think success is a thing worth having. You have been wrong in all that you taught me, mother, quite wrong. Lord Illingworth is a successful man. He is a fashionable man. He is a man who lives in the world and for it. Well, I would give anything to be just like Lord Illingworth.

MRS ARBUTHNOT

I would sooner see you dead.

GERALD

Mother, what is your objection to Lord Illingworth? Tell me – tell me right out. What is it?

MRS ARBUTHNOT

He is a bad man.

GERALD

In what way bad? I don't understand what you mean.

MRS ARBUTHNOT

I will tell you.

GERALD

I suppose you think him bad, because he doesn't believe the same things as you do. Well, men are different from women, mother. It is natural that they should have different views.

MRS ARBUTHNOT

It is not what Lord Illingworth believes, or what he does not believe, that makes him bad. It is what he is.

397–8 *I think society must be exquisite* LC, etc. (I think society must be exquisite. I long to go into it BLMS). Compare Gerald's speech with the lessons on success, power and wealth learned from Baron Arnheim by Sir Robert Chiltern (*Husband*, II, 91–109).

404 *I would sooner see you dead* LC, etc. (Aleck, don't say that. I would sooner see you dead than like him BLMS).

408 *I don't understand what you mean* (om. LC, T).

410–2 *he doesn't believe ... should have different views* LC, BLii (he doesn't believe all the old conventionalities one has been taught about life. He is perfectly right. There is not one of them that is not unsound, illogical, ridiculous BLMS; he doesn't believe all the things one has been taught about life BLi).

412 *have different views* LC, BLii (be brought up differently T).

GERALD
Mother, is it something you know of him? Something you actually know?

MRS ARBUTHNOT
It is something I know.

GERALD
Something you are quite sure of?

MRS ARBUTHNOT
Quite sure of.

GERALD
How long have you known it?

MRS ARBUTHNOT
For twenty years.

GERALD
Is it fair to go back twenty years in any man's career? And what have you or I to do with Lord Illingworth's early life? What business is it of ours?

MRS ARBUTHNOT
What this man has been, he is now, and will be always.

GERALD
Mother, tell me what Lord Illingworth did? If he did anything shameful, I will not go away with him. Surely you know me well enough for that?

MRS ARBUTHNOT
Gerald, come near to me. Quite close to me, as you used to do when you were a little boy, when you were mother's own boy. (GERALD *sits down beside his mother. She runs her fingers through his hair, and strokes his hands*) Gerald, there was a girl once, she was very young, she was little over eighteen at the time. George Harford – that was Lord Illingworth's name then – George Harford met her. She knew nothing about life.

416 *actually know?* BLMS adds here: 'Or is it merely some silly bit of second-hand gossip. If he is a bad man, as you say, I would not go away with him. But . . . but is it something you *know?*'

424 *What business is it of ours?* this speech is much longer in BLMS and goes on:
I have often heard you say that we should all be more charitable one about another. And you have always been so charitable yourself about people, mother. You have always said that it is unfair to judge people by their pasts. And if anyone has done anything wrong, you have always been the one to find excuses for them, and to say that they are going to lead a better life, and that sort of thing. Why are you so hard on Lord Illingworth?

430–1 *when you were your mother's own boy* BLii, etc. (del. T; om. LC).

He – knew everything. He made this girl love him. He made her love him so much that she left her father's house with him one morning. She loved him so much, and he had promised to marry her! He had solemnly promised to marry her, and she had believed him. She was very young, and – and ignorant of what life really is. But he put the marriage off from week to week, and month to month. – She trusted in him all the while. She loved him. – Before her child was born – for she had a child – she implored him for the child's sake to marry her, that the child might have a name, that her sin might not be visited on the child, who was innocent. He refused. After the child was born she left him, taking the child away, and her life was ruined, and her soul ruined, and all that was sweet, and good, and pure in her ruined also. She suffered terribly – she suffers now. She will always suffer. For her there is no joy, no peace, no atonement. She is a woman who drags a chain like a guilty thing. She is a woman who wears a mask, like a thing that is a leper. The fire cannot purify her. The waters cannot quench her anguish. Nothing can heal her! no anodyne can give her sleep! no poppies forgetfulness! She is lost! She is a lost soul! – That is why I call Lord Illingworth a bad man. That is why I don't want my boy to be with him.

GERALD

My dear mother, it all sounds very tragic, of course. But I dare say the girl was just as much to blame as Lord Illingworth was. – After all, would a really nice girl, a girl with any nice feelings at all, go away from her home with a man to whom she was not married, and live with him as his wife? No nice girl would.

MRS ARBUTHNOT (*After a pause*)

Gerald, I withdraw all my objections. You are at liberty to go away with Lord Illingworth, when and where you choose.

438 *one morning*. BLMS has a further sentence at this point specifying the length of the illicit relationship: 'She stayed with him for a year abroad.'

439–40 *He had solemnly . . . had believed him* BLii, etc. (del. T; om. LC).

453 *a leper* (plague-stricken T, BLii, BLi).

453–4 *The fire cannot purify her. The waters cannot quench her anguish* (The fire cannot purify her and make her clean of stain. The waters cannot quench her anguish and bring her peace BLMS).

455 *poppies* i.e. opium, derived from one species of poppy (*Papaver somniferum*). Dorian Gray frequents opium dens in the East End of London.

459 *tragic* (dreadful LC, etc.).

463–4 *No nice girl would* (No nice girl would. I should fancy it was extremely probable the young girl in question was no better than she should have been LC, etc.).

GERALD
Dear mother, I knew you wouldn't stand in my way. You are the best woman God ever made. And, as for Lord Illingworth, I don't believe he is capable of anything infamous or base. I can't believe it of him – I can't.

HESTER (*Outside*)
Let me go! Let me go!

Enter HESTER *in terror, and rushes over to* GERALD *and flings herself in his arms*

HESTER
Oh! save me – save me from him!

GERALD
From whom?

HESTER
He has insulted me! Horribly insulted me! Save me!

GERALD
Who? Who has dared – ?

LORD ILLINGWORTH *enters at back of stage.* HESTER *breaks from* GERALD'*s arms and points to him*

GERALD (*He is quite beside himself with rage and indignation*)
Lord Illingworth, you have insulted the purest thing on God's earth, a thing as pure as my own mother. You have insulted the woman I love most in the world with my own mother. As there is a God in heaven, I will kill you!

MRS ARBUTHNOT (*Rushing across and catching hold of him*)
No! no!

GERALD (*Thrusting her back*)
Don't hold me, mother. Don't hold me – I'll kill him!

MRS ARBUTHNOT
Gerald!

GERALD
Let me go, I say!

468 *God ever made* C, BLMS (in the whole world LC, T, BLii, BLi).
468–70 *And as for Lord Illingworth . . . I can't* (om. LC, etc.).
471 *Let me go! Let me go!* BLi, etc. (Let me go! Let me go! GERALD [*starting*]: What is that? LC, T, BLii).
475 s.d. (om. LC, etc.).
477 *a thing as pure as my own mother* LC, etc. (except my mother BLMS). C, BLMS add the following sentence: 'You are infamous. You are foul, You are polluted.'
483 *Let me go, I say!* (Let me go, I say! Don't hold me like that! T, BLii).

MRS ARBUTHNOT

Stop, Gerald, stop! He is your own father!

GERALD *clutches his mother's hands and looks into her face. She sinks slowly on the ground in shame.* HESTER *steals towards the door.* LORD ILLINGWORTH *frowns and bites his lip. After a time* GERALD *raises his mother up, puts his arm round her, and leads her from the room*

ACT DROP

Fourth Act

Scene – Sitting-room at MRS ARBUTHNOT'S
Large open French window at back, looking on to garden. Doors R.C. and L.C.
GERALD ARBUTHNOT *writing at table*
Enter ALICE *R.C. followed by* LADY HUNSTANTON *and* MRS ALLONBY

ALICE

Lady Hunstanton and Mrs Allonby. *Exit L.C.*

LADY HUNSTANTON

Good morning, Gerald.

GERALD (*Rising*)

Good morning, Lady Hunstanton. Good morning, Mrs Allonby.

LADY HUNSTANTON (*Sitting down*)

We came to inquire for your dear mother, Gerald. I hope she is better?

GERALD

My mother has not come down yet, Lady Hunstanton.

LADY HUNSTANTON

Ah, I am afraid the heat was too much for her last night. I

484 s.d. ([MRS ARBUTHNOT *sinks on her knees and bows her head.* HESTER *with a look of pain glides from the room.* LORD ILLINGWORTH *bites his lip, hesitates for a moment, and then goes off.* GERALD *forces his mother back, and with a look of horror and amazement, gazes into her face*] LC, T, BLii; om. BLi).

3–4 *Good morning, Mrs Allonby* BLMS has the following additional speech for Mrs Al:

MRS AL

Good morning, Mr Arbuthnot. How serious you look! You must be trying to understand some of Lord Illingworth's aphorisms about life. It's quite hopeless, I assure you. I gave up making the attempt months ago. Lord Illingworth is the one incomprehensible left to us in this commonplace age.

think there must have been thunder in the air. Or perhaps it was the music. Music makes one feel so romantic – at least it always gets on one's nerves.

MRS ALLONBY
It's the same thing, nowadays.

LADY HUNSTANTON
I am so glad I don't know what you mean, dear. I am afraid you mean something wrong. Ah, I see you're examining Mrs Arbuthnot's pretty room. Isn't it nice and old-fashioned?

MRS ALLONBY (*Surveying the room through her lorgnette*)
It looks quite the happy English home.

LADY HUNSTANTON
That's just the word, dear; that just describes it. One feels your mother's good influence in everything she has about her, Gerald.

MRS ALLONBY
Lord Illingworth says that all influence is bad, but that a good influence is the worst in the world.

LADY HUNSTANTON
When Lord Illingworth knows Mrs Arbuthnot better, he will change his mind. I must certainly bring him here.

MRS ALLONBY
I should like to see Lord Illingworth in a happy English home.

LADY HUNSTANTON
It would do him a great deal of good, dear. Most women in

9 *thunder in the air* BLii, BLMS add here: 'I am sure there was thunder in the air.'
10–13 *Music makes one feel . . . what you mean, dear* (del. T; om. LC).
13–14 *I am afraid you mean something wrong* see Appendix I.
17 *that just describes it* BLii, BLMS add here: 'A happy English home! I like this room so much.'
18 *everything she has about her, Gerald* LC adds here: 'I must certainly bring Lord Brancaster here.'
20–1 *Lord Illingworth says . . . in the world* another sentiment that Wilde used first in *Dorian Gray*: 'There is no such thing as a good influence, Mr Gray. All influence is immoral — immoral from the scientific point of view.' (*DG*, p. 17/*CW*, p. 28.)
22–3 *knows Mrs Arbuthnot better, he will change his mind* T, etc. (doesn't know Mrs Arbuthnot yet. He has only seen her once. When he knows her better, which I hope he will do, he will change his mind C, BLii, BLMS).
24–5 *in a happy English home*. BLii, BLMS add here: 'It would be such a new experience for him.'
26 *a great deal of good, dear* BLii, C, BLMS add here: 'Poor dear Hunstanton used to say that rooms were exactly like the people who lived in them. I hope, by the way, that is not always the case.'

London, nowadays, seem to furnish their rooms with nothing but orchids, foreigners, and French novels. But here we have the room of a sweet saint. Fresh natural flowers, books that don't shock one, pictures that one can look at without blushing.

MRS ALLONBY
But I like blushing.

LADY HUNSTANTON
Well, there *is* a good deal to be said for blushing, if one can do it at the proper moment. Poor dear Hunstanton used to tell me I didn't blush nearly often enough. But then he was so very particular. He wouldn't let me know any of his men friends, except those who were over seventy, like poor Lord Ashton: who afterwards, by the way, was brought into the Divorce Court. A most unfortunate case.

MRS ALLONBY
I delight in men over seventy. They always offer one the devotion of a lifetime. I think seventy an ideal age for a man.

LADY HUNSTANTON
She is quite incorrigible, Gerald, isn't she? By-the-by, Gerald, I hope your dear mother will come and see me more often

29 *Fresh natural flowers* BLii, BLMS add here: 'not like those horrid dyed things that James always wears in his buttonhole.' There is a private joke here. Wilde's early reputation had been acquired by appearing to cultivate the artificial and he reputedly came on stage after the first night of *Lady Windermere's Fan* wearing a green carnation. Some of Lady H's sentiments derive from *Dorian Gray*: 'I can't afford orchids, but I spare no expense in foreigners. They make one's rooms look so picturesque.' (*DG*, p. 45/*CW*, p. 47.)

35–6 *he was so very particular* BLii and BLMS add here: 'He had such high standards. He never introduced me to *one* of his female friends and as for his men friends, he wouldn't let me know any of them.'

37 *Ashton* (Cromer BLii, C, BLMS; Dawlish LC, T, BLi). These details of name changes are one of the few means of dating the drafts. Much of the first draft of the play was written while Wilde was at Cromer, hence the use of Norfolk place names generally in the play and specifically here. However Evelyn Baring was created Lord Cromer of Cromer on 20 June 1893 and Wilde changed the name of the character to Dawlish. (Wilde seems to have known or known of the Cromer family: see *Letters*, p. 346.) Dawlish is the name of a resort in Devon. The reasons for Wilde's further revision to Ashton are unclear; ironically, however, after the first edition had been published James Williamson, formerly MP for Lancaster, was created Baron Ashton.

40 *They always offer* LC, etc. (They take such pains to be dangerous and then they always offer BLii, BLMS).

41 *devotion of a lifetime* all drafts add here: 'That is so very gratifying.'

43 *She is quite . . . isn't she?* see Appendix I.

44–5 *more often now* (more often now that she is going to be alone LC, etc.).

now. You and Lord Illingworth start almost immediately, don't you?

GERALD
I have given up my intention of being Lord Illingworth's secretary.

LADY HUNSTANTON
Surely not, Gerald! It would be most unwise of you. What reason can you have?

GERALD
I don't think I should be suitable for the post.

MRS ALLONBY
I wish Lord Illingworth would ask me to be his secretary. But he says I am not serious enough.

LADY HUNSTANTON
My dear, you really mustn't talk like that in this house. Mrs Arbuthnot doesn't know anything about the wicked society in which we all live. She won't go into it. She is far too good. I consider it was a great honour her coming to me last night. It gave quite an atmosphere of respectability to the party.

MRS ALLONBY
Ah, that must have been what you thought was thunder in the air.

LADY HUNSTANTON
My dear, how can you say that? There is no resemblance between the two things at all. But really, Gerald, what do you mean by not being suitable?

GERALD
Lord Illingworth's views of life and mine are too different.

LADY HUNSTANTON
But, my dear Gerald, at your age you shouldn't have any views

51 *I don't think* in BLMS Wilde mistakenly retained the name of Aleck rather than Gerald in the attribution of this speech. See 'The Play, Its Drafts and Genesis'.
52 *ask me to be his secretary* see Appendix I.
54 *like that in this house* BLii, C, BLMS add here: 'If Mrs Arbuthnot was here she'd be quite shocked. Wouldn't she, Gerald?'
63 *by not being suitable*? BLii, BLMS add here: 'Why to be a private secretary nowadays, you needn't know anything. You needn't even know how to spell. James could be a private secretary. And his spelling is the most daring thing possible. The amount of letters James gets into a word is quite extraordinary. And he won't be taught. He says it's not good form to spell well.'

of life. They are quite out of place. You must be guided by others in this matter. Lord Illingworth has made you the most flattering offer, and travelling with him you would see the world – as much of it, at least, as one should look at – under the best auspices possible, and stay with all the right people, which is so important at this solemn moment in your career.

GERALD
I don't want to see the world: I've seen enough of it.

MRS ALLONBY
I hope you don't think you have exhausted life, Mr Arbuthnot. When a man says that one knows that life has exhausted him.

GERALD
I don't wish to leave my mother.

LADY HUNSTANTON
Now, Gerald, that is pure laziness on your part. Not leave your mother! If I were your mother I would insist on your going.

Enter ALICE *L.C.*

ALICE
Mrs Arbuthnot's compliments, my lady, but she has a bad headache, and cannot see any one this morning.

Exit R.C.

LADY HUNSTANTON (*Rising*)
A bad headache! I am so sorry! Perhaps you'll bring her up to Hunstanton this afternoon, if she is better, Gerald.

GERALD
I am afraid not this afternoon, Lady Hunstanton.

66–7 *You must be guided by others in this matter* (I assure you James has no views of life at all. He doesn't think on the subject. No, Gerald, you must be guided by others in this matter BLii, BLMS; del. T; om. LC).
70–2 *and stay with all . . . in your career* (del. T; om. LC).
78 *laziness on your part* BLii, BLMS add here: 'Really, you young men of the present day have no ambition at all. It all goes in cigarettes, I believe, except what is left for late hours.'
79–80 *insist on your going* see Appendix I.
80 s.d. in BLMS Wilde used the name of Rachel instead of Alice, forgetting presumably that he had already used the name for Mrs Arbuthnot.
83 *A bad headache*! see Appendix I.
84 *if she is better, Gerald* LC, etc. (I won't let you throw away such a chance without talking seriously to her about it BLMS; if she is better, Gerald. I won't let you throw away such a chance without talking seriously to her about it BLii, C).

LADY HUNSTANTON
Well, tomorrow, then. Ah, if you had a father, Gerald, he wouldn't let you waste your life here. He would send you off with Lord Illingworth at once. But mothers are so weak. They give up to their sons in everything. We are all heart, all heart. Come, dear, I must call at the rectory and inquire for Mrs Daubeny, who, I am afraid, is far from well. It is wonderful how the Archdeacon bears up, quite wonderful. He is the most sympathetic of husbands. Quite a model. Good-bye, Gerald, give my fondest love to your mother.

MRS ALLONBY
Good-bye, Mr Arbuthnot.

GERALD
Good-bye.

Exit LADY HUNSTANTON *and* MRS ALLONBY
GERALD *sits down and reads over his letter*

GERALD
What name can I sign? I, who have no right to any name.

Signs name, puts letter into envelope, addresses it, and is about to seal it, when door L.C. opens and MRS ARBUTHNOT *enters.* GERALD *lays down sealing-wax.* MOTHER *and* SON *look at each other*

LADY HUNSTANTON (*Through French window at the back*)
Good-bye again, Gerald. We are taking the short cut across your pretty garden. Now, remember my advice to you – start at once with Lord Illingworth.

MRS ALLONBY
Au revoir, Mr Arbuthnot. Mind you bring me back something nice from your travels – not an Indian shawl – on no account an Indian shawl. *Exeunt*

GERALD
Mother, I have just written to him.

86 *Well, tomorrow, then* LC, T add here: 'What nice books your mother has! All written by Archdeacons or Colonial Bishops. That makes one feel so safe, doesn't it?'
90–3 *Come, dear, I must ... Good-bye* see Appendix I.
96 s.d. T, etc. (om. LC).
100 *at once with Lord Illingworth* (at once with Lord Illingworth. Your whole career depends on him. Remember that LC, T, BLi). BLii and BLMS have a much longer speech: 'If your mother is a sensible woman, as indeed I know she is, she should pack up your things immediately. Lord Illingworth is one of the most distinguished men of the day, and she must be very proud that he takes such an interest in you, very proud indeed.'

MRS ARBUTHNOT
To whom?

GERALD
To my father. I have written to tell him to come here at four o'clock this afternoon.

MRS ARBUTHNOT
He shall not come here. He shall not cross the threshold of my house.

GERALD
He must come.

MRS ARBUTHNOT
Gerald, if you are going away with Lord Illingworth, go at once. Go before it kills me: but don't ask me to meet him.

GERALD
Mother, you don't understand. Nothing in the world would induce me to go away with Lord Illingworth, or to leave you. Surely you know me well enough for that. No: I have written to him to say –

MRS ARBUTHNOT
What can you have to say to him?

GERALD
Can't you guess, mother, what I have written in this letter?

MRS ARBUTHNOT
No.

GERALD
Mother, surely you can. Think, think what must be done, now, at once, within the next few days.

MRS ARBUTHNOT
There is nothing to be done.

GERALD
I have written to Lord Illingworth to tell him that he must marry you.

MRS ARBUTHNOT
Marry me?

108–10 *He shall not come . . . He must come* BLii, etc. (om. T, LC).
108–9 *threshold of my house* BLii, BLMS add: 'I will not see him again.'
112 *ask me to meet him* BLii, BLMS add here: 'Was last night not enough in all its shame and horror?'

GERALD

Mother, I will force him to do it. The wrong that has been done you must be repaired. Atonement must be made. Justice may be slow, mother, but it comes in the end. In a few days you shall be Lord Illingworth's lawful wife.

MRS ARBUTHNOT

But, Gerald –

GERALD

I will insist upon his doing it. I will make him do it: he will not dare to refuse.

MRS ARBUTHNOT

But, Gerald, it is I who refuse. I will not marry Lord Illingworth.

GERALD

Not marry him? Mother!

MRS ARBUTHNOT

I will not marry him.

GERALD

But you don't understand: it is for your sake I am talking, not for mine. This marriage, this necessary marriage, this marriage that, for obvious reasons, must inevitably take place, will not help me, will not give me a name that will be really, rightly mine to bear. But surely it will be something for you, that you, my mother, should, however late, become the wife of the man who is my father. Will not that be something?

MRS ARBUTHNOT

I will not marry him.

GERALD

Mother, you must.

MRS ARBUTHNOT

I will not. You talk of atonement for a wrong done. What

126 *force him to do it* see Appendix I.

127–8 *Justice may be slow, mother, but it comes in the end* LC, etc. (Justice may be slow, mother, but it comes in the end. Crooked things are made straight; things that are evil are set right at last BLii; om. T).

142 *the wife* BLii, etc. (the lawful wife LC, T).

145 *you must* BLii, BLMS (you can't mean what you say LC, etc.).

146–7 *What atonement can be made to me*? LC, etc. (What atonement can be made to me for the mask I have had to wear, and the misery that made me wear it? C; What atonement can be made to me for the shame I have suffered, for the secret I have hid, for the mask I have had to wear, and the misery that made me wear it? Atonement? BLii, BLMS). Wilde may have deleted the lines because of their closeness to Mrs Erlynne's in Act IV of *LWF*.

atonement can be made to me? There is no atonement possible. I am disgraced: he is not. That is all. It is the usual history of a man and a woman as it usually happens, as it always happens. And the ending is the ordinary ending. The woman suffers. The man goes free.

GERALD

I don't know if that is the ordinary ending, mother: I hope it is not. But your life, at any rate, shall not end like that. The man shall make whatever reparation is possible. It is not enough. It does not wipe out the past, I know that. But at least it makes the future better, better for you, mother.

MRS ARBUTHNOT

I refuse to marry Lord Illingworth.

GERALD

If he came to you himself and asked you to be his wife you would give him a different answer. Remember, he is my father.

MRS ARBUTHNOT

If he came himself, which he will not do, my answer would be the same. Remember I am your mother.

GERALD

Mother, you make it terribly difficult for me by talking like that, and I can't understand why you won't look at this matter from the right, from the only proper standpoint. It is to take away the bitterness out of your life, to take away the shadow that lies on your name, that this marriage must take place. There is no alternative: and after the marriage you and I can go away together. But the marriage must take place first. It is a duty that you owe, not merely to yourself, but to all other women – yes: to all the other women in the world, lest he betray more.

MRS ARBUTHNOT

I owe nothing to other women. There is not one of them to help me. There is not one woman in the world to whom I could go for pity, if I would take it, or for sympathy, if I could win

154–5 *It is not enough* (It may not be enough. It is not enough BLii, BLMS).
154–6 *It is not enough . . . better for you, mother* (del. T; om. LC).
158 *If he came* BLMS (Mother, if he came LC, T, BLii, C, BLi).
161 *If he came himself* LC, etc. (If your father came BLii, C, BLMS).
161–2 *answer would be the same* here BLii, C, BLMS add: 'I would rather lie in the grave than be George Harbord's wife.'
163–9 *Mother, you make . . . take place first* (del. T; om. LC).
173–6 *There is not . . . win it* (del. T; om. LC).

it. Women are hard on each other. That girl, last night, good though she is, fled from the room as though I were a tainted thing. She was right. I am a tainted thing. But my wrongs are my own, and I will bear them alone. I must bear them alone. What have women who have not sinned to do with me, or I with them? We do not understand each other.

Enter HESTER *behind*

GERALD
I implore you to do what I ask you.

MRS ARBUTHNOT
What son has ever asked of his mother to make so hideous a sacrifice? None.

GERALD
What mother has ever refused to marry the father of her own child? None.

MRS ARBUTHNOT
Let me be the first, then. I will not do it.

GERALD
Mother, you believe in religion, and you brought me up to believe in it also. Well, surely your religion, the religion that you taught me when I was a boy, mother, must tell you that I am right. You know it, you feel it.

MRS ARBUTHNOT
I do not know it. I do not feel it, nor will I ever stand before God's altar and ask God's blessing on so hideous a mockery as a marriage between me and George Harford. I will not say the words the Church bids us to say. I will not say them. I dare not. How could I swear to love the man I loathe, to honour him who wrought you dishonour, to obey him who, in his mastery, made me to sin? No: marriage is a sacrament for those who love each other. It is not for such as him, or such

176 *good* LC, etc. (gentle and good BLii, BLMS).
182 *I implore you to do what I ask you* (Mother, don't say that. MRS AR: Why should I not say it? It is true. GERALD: It is not true and I implore you to do what I ask you BLii, BLMS).
188 *Mother, you believe* LC, etc. (But — don't turn away from me, mother. Do listen to what I have to say. It is only right you should listen. Mother, you believe BLii, BLMS).
189 *believe in it also* BLii, BLMS add here: 'I have sometimes thought you were rather too strict about it, not merely as regards me, but — but in your own life. You seemed to give nearly all that was in you to religion, and that sort of thing.'
191 *you feel it* BLii, BLMS add here: 'You can't help feeling it.'
194–8 *I will not say . . . to sin? No*: (del. T; om. LC).

as me. Gerald, to save you from the world's sneers and taunts I have lied to the world. For twenty years I have lied to the world. I could not tell the world the truth. Who can, ever? But not for my own sake will I lie to God, and in God's presence. No, Gerald, no ceremony, Church-hallowed or State-made, shall ever bind me to George Harford. It may be that I am too bound to him already, who, robbing me, yet left me richer, so that in the mire of my life, I found the pearl of price, or what I thought would be so.

GERALD

I don't understand you now.

MRS ARBUTHNOT

Men don't understand what mothers are. I am no different from other women except in the wrong done me and the wrong I did, and my very heavy punishments and great disgrace. And yet, to bear you I had to look on death. To nurture you I had to wrestle with it. Death fought with me for you. All women have to fight with death to keep their children. Death, being childless, wants our children from us. Gerald, when you were naked I clothed you, when you were hungry I gave you food. Night and day all that long winter I tended you. No office is too mean, no care too lowly for the thing we women love – and oh! how *I* loved *you*. Not Hannah Samuel more. And you needed love, for you were weakly, and only love could have kept you alive. Only love can keep any one alive. And boys are careless often and without thinking give pain, and we always fancy that when they come to man's estate and know us better, they will repay us. But it is not so.

207 *so that in the mire* LC, etc. (so that from my ruin came my joy, and in the mire BLii, BLMS).

208 *or what I thought would be so* LC, etc. (om. BLMS).

217 *Gerald, when you were naked* cf. *Matthew* 25.35-6: 'For I was hungry, and you gave me to eat: I was thirsty, and you gave me to drink: I was a stranger, and you took me in: naked, and you covered me; sick, and you visited me: I was in prison, and you came to me.'

218 *I gave you food* BLii, BLMS add here: 'When you were cold I warmed you. If you were sleepless I walked with you all night long in my arms. If you were fretful I made songs to soothe you, singing with lips dry with pain or laughing that you might not see my tears.'

220 *Hannah* i.e. the mother of the prophet Samuel; traditionally a model for both religious piety and maternal affection. See I *Kings*, 1-2.

222–3 *keep anyone alive* BLii, C, BLMS add here: 'And then you began to grow up, and became stronger, oh! much stronger, and ran about, and wanted playmates. And I felt you would be happier at school than you were at home. It was dull for you here, with only me to talk to, and so I sent you to school and was glad if you wrote me a blotted boyish scrawl once in a term, something that I sitting alone in twilight might kiss and kiss again.'

224–5 *when they come to man's estate* from Feste's last song in *Twelfth Night* (V.i, 413).

The world draws them from our side, and they make friends with whom they are happier than they are with us, and have amusements from which we are barred, and interests that are not ours: and they are unjust to us often, for when they find life bitter they blame us for it, and when they find it sweet we do not taste its sweetness with them... You made many friends and went into their houses and were glad with them, and I, knowing my secret, did not dare to follow, but stayed at home and closed the door, shut out the sun and sat in darkness. What should I have done in honest households? My past was ever with me... And you thought I didn't care for the pleasant things of life. I tell you I longed for them, but did not dare to touch them, feeling I had no right. You thought I was happier working amongst the poor. That was my mission, you imagined. It was not, but where else was I to go? The sick do not ask if the hand that smooths their pillow is pure, nor the dying care if the lips that touch their brow have known the kiss of sin. It was you I thought of all the time; I gave to them the love you did not need: lavished on them a love that was not theirs... And you thought I spent too much of my time in going to Church, and in Church duties. But where else could I turn? God's house is the only house where sinners are made welcome, and you were always in my heart, Gerald, too much in my heart. For, though day after day, at morn or evensong, I have knelt in God's house, I have never repented of my sin. How could I repent of my sin when you, my love, were its fruit! Even now that you are bitter to me I cannot repent. I do not. You are more to me than innocence. I would rather be your mother – oh! much rather! – than have been always pure... Oh, don't you see? don't you understand? It is my dishonour that has made you so dear to me. It is my disgrace that has bound you so closely to me. It is the price I paid for you – the price of soul and body – that makes me love you as I do. Oh, don't ask me to do this horrible thing. Child of my shame, be still the child of my shame!

GERALD

Mother, I didn't know you loved me so much as that. And I

235–6 *My past was ever with me* (del. T; om. LC).
238–45 *You thought I was . . . was not theirs* (del. T; om. LC).
246–7 *and in Church duties. But where else could I turn*? LC, etc. (and when you proposed any pleasant expedition anywhere, there was always some church duty, wasn't there? that prevented my going with you — that is quite true. But where else had I to go? BLii, BLMS)
250 *evensong* the evening service in the Anglican liturgy.
252 *were its fruit*! BLii, BLMS add here: 'I worshipped you too much. I am punished for it. Why should I not be punished, seeing I cannot repent?'

will be a better son to you than I have been. And you and I must never leave each other . . . but, mother . . . I can't help it . . . you must become my father's wife. You must marry him. It is your duty.

HESTER (*Running forward and embracing* MRS ARBUTHNOT)
No, no: you shall not. That would be real dishonour, the first you have ever known. That would be real disgrace: the first to touch you. Leave him and come with me. There are other countries than England. . . Oh! other countries over sea, better, wiser, and less unjust lands. The world is very wide and very big.

MRS ARBUTHNOT
No, not for me. For me the world is shrivelled to a palm's breadth, and where I walk there are thorns.

HESTER
It shall not be so. We shall somewhere find green valleys and fresh waters, and if we weep, well, we shall weep together. Have we not both loved him?

GERALD
Hester!

HESTER (*Waving him back*)
Don't, don't! You cannot love me at all, unless you love her also. You cannot honour me, unless she's holier to you. In her all womanhood is martyred. Not she alone, but all of us are stricken in her house.

GERALD
Hester, Hester, what shall I do?

HESTER
Do you respect the man who is your father?

GERALD
Respect him? I despise him! He is infamous!

262 *than I have been* BLii, BLMS add here: 'I have no-one to love me but you, mother, now. I suppose I never had anyone but you to really love me.'
263–4 *I can't help it* T, etc. (om. LC).
269 *countries than England* BLii, BLMS add here: 'with its evil social life, its hideous pleasures and its hideous wrongs.' C is similar.
272–3 *to a palm's breadth* BLii, BLMS add here: 'For me there is no escape. My shame is ever with me.'
276 *Have we not both loved him*? BLii, etc. (Do we not both love him? LC, T, BLi).
280–1 *Not she alone . . . in her house* pseudo-biblical. The term 'house' implies the classical or biblical sense of 'kindred' or 'lineage'.
284 *He is infamous*. (He is infamous. Hester, tell me what I should do? LC; He is infamous. I would she had not stood between us last night. I might have killed him. MABEL: Oh! hush. GERALD: What shall I do? BLii, BLMS).

HESTER
I thank you for saving me from him last night.

GERALD
Ah, that is nothing. I would die to save you. But you don't tell me what to do now!

HESTER
Have I not thanked you for saving *me*?

GERALD
But what should I do?

HESTER
Ask your own heart, not mine. I never had a mother to save, or shame.

MRS ARBUTHNOT
He is hard – he is hard. Let me go away.

GERALD (*Rushes over and kneels down beside his mother*)
Mother, forgive me: I have been to blame.

MRS ARBUTHNOT
Don't kiss my hands: they are cold. My heart is cold: something has broken it.

HESTER
Ah, don't say that. Hearts live by being wounded. Pleasure may turn a heart to stone, riches may make it callous, but sorrow – oh, sorrow cannot break it. Besides, what sorrows have you now? Why, at this moment you are more dear to him than ever, *dear* though you have *been*, and oh! how dear you *have* been always. Ah! be kind to him.

GERALD
You are my mother and my father all in one. I need no second parent. It was for you I spoke, for you alone. Oh, say something, mother. Have I but found one love to lose another? Don't tell me that. O mother, you are cruel.

Gets up and flings himself sobbing on a sofa

MRS ARBUTHNOT (*To* HESTER)
But has he found indeed another love?

286–7 *Ah! that is nothing . . . to do now*! (You don't tell me what to do! BLii, BLMS).
289 *But what should I do*? BLi adds here: 'Hester, tell me what should I do?'
301 *Ah! be kind to him* (del. T; om. LC).
302 *You are my mother* LC, etc. (I have been to blame. But it was not of myself that I was thinking. Ah! don't imagine that. I am content. You are my mother BLii, BLMS).

HESTER
You know I have loved him always.

MRS ARBUTHNOT
But we are very poor.

HESTER
Who, being loved, is poor? Oh, no one. I hate my riches. They are a burden. Let him share it with me.

MRS ARBUTHNOT
But we are disgraced. We rank among the outcasts. Gerald is nameless. The sins of the parents should be visited on the children. It is God's law.

HESTER
I was wrong. God's law is only Love.

MRS ARBUTHNOT (*Rises, and taking* HESTER *by the hand, goes slowly over to where* GERALD *is lying on the sofa with his head buried in his hands. She touches him and he looks up*)
Gerald, I cannot give you a father, but I have brought you a wife.

GERALD
Mother, I am not worthy either of her or you.

MRS ARBUTHNOT
So she comes first, you are worthy. And when you are away, Gerald ... with ... her – oh, think of me sometimes. Don't forget me. And when you pray, pray for me. We should pray when we are happiest, and you will be happy, Gerald.

HESTER
Oh, you don't think of leaving us?

GERALD
Mother, you won't leave us?

308 *But we are very poor* LC, etc. (But we are very poor, poorer than Gerald thinks. I work for hire, sewing BLii, BLMS).
312–3 *The sins of the parents ... on the children* (We have no name that is our own BLii, BLMS; The sins of the parents should be visited on the children. It is a just law LC, T, BLi).
314 *I was wrong ... only Love* LC, etc. (You forgot God once, so God sent you Gerald that you might not again forget Him BLii, BLMS).
317 *either of her or you* C, BLii (or of her, or you LC, etc.). This archaism of style in LC was noted by many reviewers of the first production.
318–26 *And when ... near you always* (del. T; om. LC).
319–20 *Don't forget me* (If I forgot God once, oh! don't forget me BLii, BLMS).
322 *leaving us*? BLii, BLMS add here: 'You will come with us?'

MRS ARBUTHNOT
I might bring shame upon you!

GERALD
Mother!

MRS ARBUTHNOT
For a little then: and if you let me, near you always.

HESTER (*To* MRS ARBUTHNOT)
Come out with us to the garden.

MRS ARBUTHNOT
Later on, later on.

Exeunt HESTER *and* GERALD
MRS ARBUTHNOT *goes towards door L.C. Stops at looking-glass over mantlepiece and looks into it*
Enter ALICE *R.C.*

ALICE
A gentleman to see you, ma'am.

MRS ARBUTHNOT
Say I am not at home. Show me the card. (*Takes card from salver and looks at it*) Say I will not see him.

LORD ILLINGWORTH *enters.* MRS ARBUTHNOT *sees him in the glass and starts, but does not turn round*
Exit ALICE

What can you have to say to me to-day, George Harford? You can have nothing to say to me. You must leave this house.

LORD ILLINGWORTH
Rachel, Gerald knows everything about you and me now, so some arrangement must be come to that will suit us all three. I assure you, he will find in me the most charming and generous of fathers.

324 *It might bring shame on you* (I would disgrace you T, etc.).
325 *Mother*! T, BLi add here:
HESTER
Be with us. Be with us.
GERALD
Mother!
326–9 *For a little then ... see you, ma'am.* see Appendix I.
330 *Show me the card* LC, etc. (om. BLMS).
332–3 *What can you have ... leave this house* (LORD I: Leave us. Don't you hear me? MRS AR: That will do. (*Exit* ALICE) What can you have to say to me today, George Harbord? You can have nothing to say to me. You must leave this house BLii, BLMS; del. T; om. LC).
336 *I assure you* (I assure you, though you may not believe it LC, BLi).
336 *charming* (affectionate LC, etc.).

MRS ARBUTHNOT
My son may come in at any moment. I saved you last night. I may not be able to save you again. My son feels my dishonour strongly, terribly strongly. I beg you to go.

LORD ILLINGWORTH (*Sitting down*)
Last night was excessively unfortunate. That silly Puritan girl making a scene merely because I wanted to kiss her. What harm is there in a kiss?

MRS ARBUTHNOT (*Turning round*)
A kiss may ruin a human life, George Harford. *I* know that. *I* know that too well.

LORD ILLINGWORTH
We won't discuss that at present. What is of importance to-day, as yesterday, is still our son. I am extremely fond of him, as you know, and odd though it may seem to you, I admired his conduct last night immensely. He took up the cudgels for that pretty prude with wonderful promptitude. He is just what I should have liked a son of mine to be. Except that no son of mine should ever take the side of the Puritans: that is always an error. Now, what I propose is this.

MRS ARBUTHNOT
Lord Illingworth, no proposition of yours interests me.

LORD ILLINGWORTH
According to our ridiculous English laws, I can't legitimise Gerald. But I can leave him my property. Illingworth is entailed, of course, but it is a tedious barrack of a place. He

339–40 *My son feels . . . you to go* BLii, etc. (You had better go T, LC).
341 *That silly Puritan girl* LC, etc. (That Puritan girl with her old-fashioned New England notions BLii).
342 *merely because I wanted to kiss her* (del. T; om. LC).
346 *We won't discuss . . . at present* (om. LC).
347–8 *fond of him, as you know* BLii etc. (fond of Gerald, more fond of him than I ever thought I should be of anybody, or anything LC, T, BLi).
349–53 *He took up the cudgels . . . always an error* (del. T; om. LC). BLi adds here: 'But I can soon cure him of it.' BLii, C, BLMS add: 'But I can soon cure him of it. It doesn't run in our family to take the Puritan side of things.'
350 *with wonderful promptitude*. BLii, BLMS add here: 'He has got spirit and stuff in him. He is full of pluck.'
355 *According to our ridiculous* LC, etc. (Then you are a very bad mother, Rachel. It should interest you. Just listen. According to our ridiculous BLii, BLMS).
355–6 *legitimise Gerald* BLii, BLMS add here: 'I can't make him legally my son, and I can't leave him my title.'
357 *entailed* 'settled on a number of persons in succession, so that it cannot be bequeathed at pleasure by any one possessor' (*OED*).
Lord I's point is that marriage to Mrs A could legitimise *their* union, but not legitimise its issue, Gerald.
357 *barrack of a place* BLii, BLMS add here: 'Awful bore keeping it up.'

can have Ashby, which is much prettier, Harborough, which has the best shooting in the north of England, and the house in St. James's Square. What more can a gentleman desire in this world?

MRS ARBUTHNOT
Nothing more, I am quite sure.

LORD ILLINGWORTH
As for a title, a title is really rather a nuisance in these democratic days. As George Harford I had everything I wanted. Now I have merely everything that other people want, which isn't nearly so pleasant. Well, my proposal is this.

MRS ARBUTHNOT
I told you I was not interested, and I beg you to go.

LORD ILLINGWORTH
The boy is to be with you for six months in the year, and with me for the other six. That is perfectly fair, is it not? You can have whatever allowance you like, and live where you choose. As for your past, no one knows anything about it except myself and Gerald. There is the Puritan, of course, the Puritan in white muslin, but she doesn't count. She couldn't tell the story without explaining that she objected to being kissed, could she? And all the women would think her a fool and the men think her a bore. And you need not be afraid that Gerald won't be my heir. I needn't tell you I have not the slightest intention of marrying.

358 *Ashby* a number of villages in Suffolk and Norfolk bear this name. None has an estate of the size intended by Wilde.

358 *Harborough* again, no specific location is intended, although the name suggests Market Harborough in Leicestershire or Harborough Magna in Warwickshire.

360 *St. James's Square* despite the imprecision with which Lord I's two country estates are located, this address places him very exactly geographically and socially among England's political and economic élite.

363–4 *these democratic days* see Appendix I. Here the specific echo is to the debate on politics between Lord I and Mr K in I, 282–6.

368 *I told you I . . . beg you to go* (del. T; om. LC).

370–7 *You can have whatever . . . think her a bore* (del. T; om. LC).

371 *live where you choose* BLii, BLMS add here: 'You can live in London if you want to. You'll have no difficulty getting into London Society. Nowadays one has merely to feed people, amuse people, or shock people, to move in the very best society.' The lines were deleted in manuscript in BLii and the final sentence moved to III, 75–6.

377 *think her a bore* BLii, BLMS add here: 'If women are not made to be kissed I don't see what they are made for — no: I see a delightful future for Gerald and a very admirable future for you.'

MRS ARBUTHNOT
You come too late. My son has no need of you. You are not necessary.

LORD ILLINGWORTH
What do you mean, Rachel?

MRS ARBUTHNOT
That you are not necessary to Gerald's career. He does not require you.

LORD ILLINGWORTH
I do not understand you.

MRS ARBUTHNOT
Look into the garden. (LORD ILLINGWORTH *rises and goes towards window*) You had better not let them see you: you bring unpleasant memories. (LORD ILLINGWORTH *looks out and starts*) She loves him. They love each other. We are safe from you, and we are going away.

LORD ILLINGWORTH
Where?

MRS ARBUTHNOT
We will not tell you, and if you find us we will not know you. You seem surprised. What welcome would you get from the girl whose lips you tried to soil, from the boy whose life you have shamed, from the mother whose dishonour comes from you?

LORD ILLINGWORTH
You have grown hard, Rachel.

MRS ARBUTHNOT
I was too weak once. It is well for me that I have changed.

LORD ILLINGWORTH
I was very young at the time. We men know life too early.

MRS ARBUTHNOT
And we women know life too late. That is the difference between men and women. *A pause*

383–4 *He does not require you* BLii, etc. (He does not require you. You can be of no use to him. LC, T, BLi).
386 *Look into the garden* (Look into the garden, Lord Illingworth. [LORD ILLINGWORTH *hesitates*] Look into the garden, Lord Illingworth T, BLi).
398 *weak* LC, etc. (pliable BLii, C, BLMS).
399 *very young* BLii, BLMS (only a boy LC, etc.).
401 s.d. A pause ([*A pause.* LORD I *pulls out cigarette case and opens it*] LORD I: Rachel! MRS AR: My son has never smoked in this room. LORD I:[*Putting cigarette case back into his pocket*] It makes no matter. MRS AR: Had you not better go, Lord Illingworth? T, BLi).

LORD ILLINGWORTH
Rachel, I want my son. My money may be of no use to him now. I may be of no use to him, but I want my son. Bring us together, Rachel. You can do it if you choose.
Sees letter on table

MRS ARBUTHNOT
There is no room in my boy's life for *you*. He is not interested in *you*.

LORD ILLINGWORTH
Then why does he write to me?

MRS ARBUTHNOT
What do you mean?

LORD ILLINGWORTH
What letter is this? *Takes up letter*

MRS ARBUTHNOT
That – is nothing. Give it to me.

LORD ILLINGWORTH
It is addressed to *me*.

MRS ARBUTHNOT
You are not to open it. I forbid you to open it.

LORD ILLINGWORTH
And in Gerald's handwriting.

MRS ARBUTHNOT
It was not to have been sent. It is a letter he wrote to you this morning before he saw me. But he is sorry now he wrote it, very sorry. You are not to open it. Give it to me.

LORD ILLINGWORTH
It belongs to me. (*Opens it, sits down and reads it slowly.* MRS ARBUTHNOT *watches him all the time*) You have read this letter, I suppose, Rachel?

MRS ARBUTHNOT
No.

411–2 *It is addressed . . . to open it* (del. T; om. LC).
413 *And in Gerald's handwriting* T, BLi add here: 'I know his handwriting.' The line refers back to a cancelled passage in Act III, where Lord I asks Gerald to write his name as Gerald Harbord. See III, 120n.
414–5 *It was not . . . he saw me* (del T; om. LC).
416 *Give it to me* (om. LC).

LORD ILLINGWORTH
You know what is in it?

MRS ARBUTHNOT
Yes!

LORD ILLINGWORTH
I don't admit for a moment that the boy is right in what he says. I don't admit that it is any duty of mine to marry you. I deny it entirely. But to get my son back I am ready – yes, I am ready to marry you, Rachel – and to treat you always with the deference and respect due to my wife. I will marry you as soon as you choose. I give you my word of honour.

MRS ARBUTHNOT
You made that promise to me once before and broke it.

LORD ILLINGWORTH
I will keep it now. And that will show you that I love my son, at least as much as you love him. For when I marry you, Rachel, there are some ambitions I shall have to surrender. High ambitions too, if any ambition is high.

MRS ARBUTHNOT
I decline to marry you, Lord Illingworth.

LORD ILLINGWORTH
Are you serious?

MRS ARBUTHNOT
Yes.

425 *I deny it entirely* BLii, BLMS add here: 'And I am bound to say that if I felt it was my duty I certainly wouldn't do it. Once one begins by doing it, one keeps on at it, one never stops, and life becomes tedious. I have known more people in this century ruined through doing their duty than through anything else. It is the vice of the age.'

426–7 *and to treat . . . to my wife* LC, etc. (om. BLii, BLMS).

430 *I will keep it now* LC, etc. (Oh! I didn't mean it then. I mean it now. I am quite ready to marry you BLii, C, BLMS).

430–3 *And that will . . . ambition is high* (del. T; om. LC). At the end of the speech, LC, T, BLi have an additional exchange:

MRS AR
So you again propose to marry me?
LORD I
I do.

434 *to marry you, Lord Illingworth* LC, T have an additional exchange here:

LORD I
You decline to marry me, Rachel?
MRS AR
I refuse.

435–8 *Are you serious . . . interest me enormously* see Appendix I.

LORD ILLINGWORTH
Do tell me your reasons. They would interest me enormously.

MRS ARBUTHNOT
I have already explained them to my son.

LORD ILLINGWORTH
I suppose they were intensely sentimental, weren't they? You women live by your emotions and for them. You have no philosophy of life.

MRS ARBUTHNOT
You are right. We women live by our emotions and for them. By our passions, and for them, if you will. I have two passions, Lord Illingworth: my love of him, my hate of you. You cannot kill those. They feed each other.

LORD ILLINGWORTH
What sort of love is that which needs to have hate as its brother?

MRS ARBUTHNOT
It is the sort of love I have for Gerald. Do you think that terrible? Well, it is terrible. All love is terrible. All love is a tragedy. I loved you once, Lord Illingworth. Oh, what a tragedy for a woman to have loved you!

LORD ILLINGWORTH
So you really refuse to marry me?

MRS ARBUTHNOT
Yes.

LORD ILLINGWORTH
Because you hate me?

MRS ARBUTHNOT
Yes.

LORD ILLINGWORTH
And does my son hate me as you do?

437–9 *They would interest . . . to my son* (del. T; om. LC).
443 *by our emotions and for them* BLii adds here: 'There is no other life for us. You men have made the world like that. By our emotions and for them!'
453 *So you really refuse to marry me*? (So you really refuse to be my wife? LC, T, BLi; You are the first woman who has ever told me so. Most women keep my memory as . . . as fondly as they keep my letters. So you really refuse to be Lady Illingworth? BLii, C, BLMS).

MRS ARBUTHNOT
No.

LORD ILLINGWORTH
I am glad of that, Rachel.

MRS ARBUTHNOT
He merely despises you.

LORD ILLINGWORTH
What a pity! What a pity for him, I mean.

MRS ARBUTHNOT
Don't be deceived, George. Children begin by loving their parents. After a time they judge them. Rarely if ever do they forgive them.

LORD ILLINGWORTH (*Reads letter over again, very slowly*)
May I ask by what arguments you made the boy who wrote this letter, this beautiful, passionate letter, believe that you should not marry his father, the father of your own child.

MRS ARBUTHNOT
It was not I who made him see it. It was another.

LORD ILLINGWORTH
What *fin-de-siècle* person?

MRS ARBUTHNOT
The Puritan, Lord Illingworth.

A pause

LORD ILLINGWORTH (*Winces, then rises slowly and goes over to table where his hat and gloves are.* MRS ARBUTHNOT *is standing close to the table. He picks up one of the gloves and begins putting it on*)
There is not much then for me to do here, Rachel?

MRS ARBUTHNOT
Nothing.

LORD ILLINGWORTH
It is good-bye, is it?

462–4 *Don't be deceived . . . forgive them* LC, etc. (om. BLii, C, BLMS). Cf. *Dorian Gray*: 'Children begin by loving their parents; as they grow older they judge them; sometimes they forgive them.' (*DG*, p. 66/*CW*, p. 61.) Cf. also II, 608–10.
466 *this beautiful, passionate letter* LC, etc. (om. BLii, BLMS).
467 *the father of your own child* LC, etc. (om. BLii, BLMS).
469 *fin-de-siècle* a phrase coined in the 1890s connoting the *avant-garde*, and hence decadence, both intellectually and morally. It was a term most usually applied to the poets and artists of the English Decadence.
472 *Nothing* BLii, etc. (There is nothing for you to do here. LC, T, BLi).

MRS ARBUTHNOT
For ever, I hope, this time, Lord Illingworth.

LORD ILLINGWORTH
How curious! At this moment you look exactly as you looked the night you left me twenty years ago. You have just the same expression in your mouth. Upon my word, Rachel, no woman ever loved me as you did. Why, you gave yourself to me like a flower, to do anything I liked with. You were the prettiest of playthings, the most fascinating of small romances... (*Pulls out watch*) Quarter to two! Must be strolling back to Hunstanton. Don't suppose I shall see you there again. I'm sorry, I am, really. It's been an amusing experience to have met amongst people of one's own rank, and treated quite seriously too, one's mistress, and one's –

MRS ARBUTHNOT *snatches up glove and strikes* LORD ILLINGWORTH *across the face with it.* LORD ILLINGWORTH *starts. He is dazed by the insult of his punishment. Then he controls himself, and goes to window and looks out at his son. Sighs, and leaves the room*

MRS ARBUTHNOT (*Falls sobbing on the sofa*)
He would have said it. He would have said it.

Enter GERALD *and* HESTER *from the garden*

GERALD
Well, dear mother. You never came out after all. So we have come in to fetch you. Mother, you have not been crying?

Kneels down beside her

MRS ARBUTHNOT
My boy! My boy! My boy!

Running her fingers through his hair

479–80 *You were the prettiest of playthings, the most fascinating of small romances* (You were the prettiest of playthings, the most adorable of all worshippers, the most fascinating of all romances. T, BLi; You were to love me forever, weren't you. You were wonderfully devoted. Till the boy came, you were the prettiest of playthings, the most fervent of worshippers, the most fascinating of small romances. Pity the boy came. Wasn't it? BLii, C, BLMS; om. LC).

485 s.d. BLMS, BLii and C have only the first sentence. In these drafts Lord I has an exit speech:

You are the woman whom I did the honour of asking to be my wife. How foolish the wisest of us are at times. But someday your son may call you by a worse name. He has my blood in his veins as well as yours. *Exit*

487–8 *You never . . . fetch you* BLi, etc. (om. BLMS, BLii).

489 *My boy! My boy! My boy*! all drafts have a further exchange following this line. LC and BLi have:

GERALD [*To* HESTER]
Darling, tear up that foolish, wrong letter of mine. It's somewhere on the table, Oh, I should never have written it, mother.

HESTER (*Coming over*)
But you have two children now. You'll let me be your daughter?

MRS ARBUTHNOT (*Looking up*)
Would you choose me for a mother?

HESTER
You of all women I have ever known.

They move towards the door leading into garden with their arms round each other's waists. GERALD *goes to table L.C. for his hat. On turning round he sees* LORD ILLINGWORTH'*s glove lying on the floor, and picks it up*

GERALD
Hallo, mother, whose glove is this? You have had a visitor. Who was it?

MRS ARBUTHNOT (*Turning round*)
Oh! no one. No one in particular. A man of no importance.

CURTAIN

HESTER *tears up the letter*

MRS AR
Hush, hush!

GERALD
I am glad I never sent it. I would not have had him read it for worlds. He is nothing to us, mother, is he?

MRS AR
My boy, my boy!

T, BLii and BLMS are similar.

490–1 *But you have . . . your daughter*? BLi, etc. (But you have two children now. Don't forget that. You'll let me be your daughter? I have no mother of my own. BLii, BLMS).

493–6 *You of all women . . . of no importance* see Appendix I.

APPENDIX I
Longer Textual Notes

I, 146–7 *I don't . . . dear Mrs Allonby* these lines were revised heavily in draft. In their place, BLMS has the following exchange:

LADY H

I am afraid, dear, you like making fools of men.

LADY C

That is never necessary.

LADY H

Men have a good time of it, Caroline.

In BLi the exchange was expanded in manuscript:

LADY H

I am afraid, dear, you like making fools of men.

LADY C

That is never necessary.

LADY H

The modern education of women is certainly wonderful. I am told nowadays that every wife knows more than her husband does.

MRS A

Much more, Lady Hunstanton. Man as a sex has been found out.

LADY H

Ah! I've found them out, too, dear, but in a different way.

This revision persists through C and BLii, where it is deleted in manuscript.

I, 246 *people who should* Lord I's speech is much more anti-democratic in the earlier drafts of the play. BLMS and BLi have the following exchange:

LORD I

I think they are the only people who should. No educated person is interested in politics.

LADY C

I wonder what Mr Kettle says of that?

SIR J

Kelvil, dear, Kelvil.

KELVIL

I consider the House of Commons to be our most admirable institution.

LORD I

I have nothing to say against the House of Commons. It is the last bulwark of our national stupidity.

The anti-democratic tone is taken up in an addition to Lord I's next speech in BLMS and BLi (and in part in T, BLii, and C):

> As for the two sides in our politics, what are they? A Radical is merely a man who hasn't dined, and a Tory simply a gentleman who has never thought. The under-fed argue with the under-educated and the result is modern legislation.

I, 421 *Charming fellow, Gerald Arbuthnot!* BLMS and BLi have a further exchange that was one of the many direct borrowings from *Dorian Gray*:

MRS AL

How you delight in disciples! What is their charm?

LORD I

It is always pleasant to have a slave to whisper in one's ear that, after all, one is immortal. But young Arbuthnot is not a disciple . . . as yet. He is simply one of the most delightful young men I have ever met.

Before the line LC and T have the following additional exchange:

[LORD I]

(*To* HESTER) Don't you think I have made a wise choice of secretary, Miss Worsley?

HESTER

I think *you* have.

I, 452–7 *What do you think . . . going to kiss her!* these lines are substantially different in C, BLi and BLMS and emphasise the sinister aspect of the challenge between Lord I and Mrs Al:

LORD I

I am not.

MRS AL

I am.

LORD I

Would you bet?

MRS AL

I don't think it is right to bet. I always lose. But I challenge you.

LORD I

I accept. You must give me some time, of course.

MRS AL

I will give you a whole week.

LORD I

A week is more than enough.

MRS AL

You will promise to tell me honestly whether you succeed or not?

LORD I

I always succeed.

The lines are omitted from LC.

I, 478–83 *Its comedy also, sometimes . . . for both of us* a substantially different and less elegant version of these lines appears in BLi and BLMS:

LORD I
Its comedy more often. But tell me what is the mysterious reason why you will always like me? I am sorry you have a reason but I may be able to do away with it.

MRS AL
I'm afraid you won't. It is that you have never made love to me.

LORD I
I thought I had.

MRS AL
Never.

LORD I
Are you quite sure?

MRS AL
How can you ask? Aren't we good friends still?

LORD I
You are quite right. I have never made love to you. I wonder why. I think our timetables did not correspond.

MRS AL
It is fortunate. There would have been a collision.

LORD I
An accident.

BLii and C are very similar but the exchange is deleted in manuscript in both.

II, 170 *compliments* BLi and BLMS have two additional speeches here that make much more explicit the innuendo behind Mrs Al's speeches:

MRS AL
He should be jealous of everyone to whom one talks, except of course, one's husband. He should be great, great friends with one's husband, that makes things so pleasant for everybody. But he should always be reminding us what martyrs we really are, for fear we might forget it, and should make us feel what a terrible thing it is to be bound by law to an unsympathetic person who doesn't understand us.

LADY C
I am bound to say I think it would be a very awkward thing for most modern wives if their husbands did understand them.

II, 212 *Lady Stutfield* BLi and BLMS have an additional exchange here:

LADY S

I am afraid the world is made for men, not for women.

MRS AL

Oh, don't say that! We have a far better time than men have. Why, there are a great many more things forbidden to us than are forbidden to them.

LADY S

Yes, that is true, quite true. I had not thought of that.

It is deleted in manuscript in BLi and moved to I, 148–52.

II, 219–21 *I think . . . dear Miss Worsley* these lines conflate elements of a much longer exchange in BLi and BLMS:

LADY H

When we were girls we were taught not to understand anything. I assure you the amount of things I and my poor dear sister were taught not to understand was quite extraordinary. I trust American education is like that.

MRS AL

I don't think it is quite the same, Lady Hunstanton. I am told that in America the young girls know everything, and the married women nothing.

LADY H

What a curious arrangement! I think I had better go over and talk to her. (*Rises and goes across to* MABEL WORSLEY) Well, dear Miss Worsley.

LADY C (*Looking round*)

Are *you* there, Miss Worsley?

MABEL

Yes, Lady Caroline.

Cf. *Husband*, I, 65, and note.

II, 231 *your guests* following this line, BLi and BLMS have an additional exchange:

LADY H

I am afraid that pretty Mrs Allenby lets her clever tongue run away with her sometimes, dear.

MABEL

Is that the only thing that Mrs Allenby allows to run away with her?

The exchange is deleted in manuscript in BLi. Cf. I, 308f.

II, 348–52 *But has Lord . . . dear* once more BLi and BLMS have a much longer exchange at this point:

MRS AR

But does Lord Illingworth really mean to make Gerald his secretary? If so, I am sure I have you to thank for it. You are always so kind to us.

LADY H

Not at all, dear. The truth is I have never even thought of such a thing. It was Lord Illingworth himself who took the greatest fancy to Aleck, and made him the offer this morning, of his own accord, which is very much better. No-one likes to be asked favours. I remember dear Lady Pagden making herself quite unpopular in London, Caroline, because she had a French governess she wanted to recommend to everyone.

LADY C

I saw the governess. Lady Pagden sent her to me. It was before Eleanor came out. She was far too good looking to be in any respectable household. I don't wonder Lady Pagden wanted to get rid of her.

LADY H

Ah, that explains it. (*To* MRS ARBUTHNOT) You don't know Lord Illingworth I believe, dear. It's the first time he's been at Hunstanton.

The lines are deleted in manuscript in BLi and elements of them moved to I, 106–15.

II, 417–8 *with his father* BLi and BLMS have a much longer exchange with these additional lines:

There had been some quarrel – I don't remember what about – some unfortunate connection, I think – but I know they didn't speak, and when they met at the Club, it was said that Sir Thomas always hid himself behind the money article in *The Times*. I am told, by the way, Caroline, that that is quite a common occurrence, nowadays, at London Clubs, and that they have to take in additional copies of *The Times* at every good Club, there are so many fathers who don't speak to their sons, and so many sons who won't have anything to do with their fathers. I think it is very much to be regretted. [. . .]

LADY C

I hope Sir John has not been drinking port, Jane. It is excessively bad for him.

LADY H

I don't think it will do him any harm, Caroline. Poor dear Hunstanton drank port every day of his life, and was all the better for it.

LADY C

But Sir John is very delicate. He requires to be carefully watched.

LADY H

You spoil him, Caroline, you do indeed.

The exchange was deleted in manuscript in BLi, but elements of Lady H's first speech were subsequently used in a speech for Lady Markby in *Husband*, II, 643–51.

II, 492 s.d. at this point BLi and BLMS have a further s.d. and an additional exchange:

(LORD I *sits gazing at* MRS ARBUTHNOT. MRS ALLENBY *chatters to him but he pays no notice*)

ALECK

Mother, why were you so cold to Lord Illingworth? One would really think that you were annoyed at his giving me the only chance I ever had in my life of doing something. Dear Mother, how pale you are. I forgot you weren't well. Let me take you home, and Lord Illingworth can come and see you tomorrow.

MRS AR

No, I will speak to him tonight. It is better.

ALECK

I do hope, mother, he won't go back on what he has said. I like him so much. There is no-one I would sooner be with than him. He is quite different from anyone else.

LADY H

Certainly, dear Doctor, we must have some music. I hope you have your violin down, Miss Worsley.

ALECK

Oh, do play. No-one plays so beautifully as you do. Let me take your violin for you.

MABEL

If you wish.

LADY H

That is very kind of you, dear.

The lines are deleted in manuscript in BLi.

II, 581–4 *from the point . . . third-rate English town* this speech is derived from a substantially longer one in BLii and BLMS:

Here is Aleck – what is his position? Well as far as the world goes, he is the son of a widow lady with a very small income – a pattern widow I am told – living in a wretched country town. My son should have a better position than that. What is his occupation? Sitting behind a ledger in a small provincial Bank from 10 till 4. Do you think that a suitable occupation for my son? What are his pleasures? A tea-party at the Rectory once a month. Cricket on Saturday afternoons with the sons of the local tradesmen. A dinner with the village doctor, who probably drinks too much or something like that. Lady Hunstanton is kind to him, when she is down here, and asks him up and that sort of thing. But the life he catches a glimpse of here, the charming people he gets to know in this house, make him hate his ordinary life, and look down on the people he usually associates with.

The omission of these lines is significant in that it focuses the interest of the play on the moral conflict rather than on the issues of social preferment.

II, 589–90 *first step . . . or a nation* (starting point in every young man's career LC, Ti; starting point in every young man's career. Before I knew who Aleck was, before I knew he even had a mother, before I had the smallest idea what close bonds bound him and me together, I made him feel how petty, how limited, how vulgar the life of a little country town is. BLii etc.)

II, 606 *Quite so* LC, Tiii, Ti, BLii add here: 'You have taught him all the old-fashioned views of life. I suppose there is not a single platitude about right and wrong that you have not dinned into his head'. The additional lines in C, BLi, BLMS are, however, longer:

You have taught him all the old moral views of life. I suppose there is not a single platitude about right and wrong that you have not dinned into his ears, not a single foolish convention that you haven't made him respect. If you had given him some of his father's philosophy of life, which you know as well as anyone, you would have done better for yourself. You hadn't the courage to do that. It was a mistake.

III, 49–57 *Oh, yes, she's always . . . going to rule* these lines underwent much revision and deletion in all the drafts. The fullest version exists in T which contains a full account of Wilde's idea of the value of dandyism. In it Lord I's speech goes on:

in spite of all the Puritans may do or say.

GERALD

The Puritans, Lord Illingworth?

LORD I

Yes, Gerald, the Puritans. Gerald, the real enemy of modern life, of every thing that makes life lovely and joyous and coloured for us, is Puritanism, and the Puritan spirit. *There* is the danger that lies ahead of the age, and most of all in England. Every now and then this England of ours finds that one of its sores shows through its rags and shrieks for the nonconformists. Caliban for nine months of the year, it is Tartuffe for the other three. Do you despise a creed that starves the body, and does not feed the soul? Why, I tell you, Gerald, that the profligate, wildest profligate who spills his life in folly, has a better, saner, finer philosophy of life than the Puritan has. He, at any rate, knows that the aim of life is the pleasure of living, and does in some way realize himself, be himself. Puritanism is the hideous survival of the self-mutilation of the savage, man in his madness making *himself* the victim of his monstrous sacrifice. Profligate, Gerald, you will never be; you will choose your pleasures too carefully, too exquisitely for that. But Puritanism you will always reject. It is not a creed for a gentleman. And, as a beginning, you will make it your ideal to be a dandy always.

Hesketh Pearson suggests that Tree objected to this passage because it was inconsistent with Lord I's other speeches in the act. (See Hesketh Pearson, *Beerbohm Tree, His Life and Laughter* (1956) p. 70.) Many of the revisions to the act, however, must have been simply on the grounds of length.

III, 105 *Far too many* LC, T (Goodness is an admirable thing, I daresay, but it is certainly not becoming. In the case of women, Gerald, I have always remarked the more principles, the less profile BLi; Oh! lots of them. They're usually asked in the evening. One doesn't meet them at dinner. At least one shouldn't. Good women are invariably ignorant women. Ignorance is the price a woman pays for being good. They're generally rather tedious to look at, also. In the case of women, Aleck, I have always remarked that the more principle, the less profile BLMS).

III, 120–33 *When one is . . . should live in it!* these lines are very different in the early drafts. T has:

LORD I

When one is in love one begins by deceiving oneself. And one ends by deceiving others. That is what the world calls a romance.

GERALD

True love must be very rare then.

LORD I (*Smiling*)

It is the privilege of people who have nothing to do. That is the one use of the idle classes in a country. As my secretary, Gerald, I am afraid you won't have nothing to do. And so, I suppose, I had better see your handwriting. A secretary's handwriting should always be susceptible of at least three interpretations. That is so important nowadays. Take a piece of paper, Gerald, and write something. Write Gerald Harford.

Passes a piece of paper across table

GERALD

Why Harford?

LORD I

That is my family name. You should study the Peerage, Gerald. It is the one book a young man about town should know thoroughly. And it is the best thing in fiction the English have ever done.

GERALD

Gerald Harford. It sounds rather nice. (*Writes it*) But I think I like Gerald Arbuthnot better. (*Writes it*) No, I like Gerald Harford the best.

LORD I

Show me. GERALD *hands him the paper*

GERALD

Yes, I wish our name had been Harford.

LORD I

Oh, Arbuthnot is a very – a very useful name. – Your handwriting is excellent, Gerald. It has not got the slightest trace of the ledger or the bank about it. It is the handwriting of a gentleman. (*Puts the paper into a pocket-book*) Gerald, you are going now into a perfectly new life with me, and I want you to know how to live.

MRS ARBUTHNOT *appears on terrace behind*

For the world has been made by fools that wise men should live in it.

BLii, BLi, BLMS are very similar.

III, 204–13 *Ah! dear Lady Stutfield . . . subject of Patagonia.* these lines underwent considerable revision and expansion through the various drafts – one of the few occasions where Wilde expanded material. BLMS has:

LADY C

John!

SIR J

Yes, my dear! *Rises and exit with* LADY CAROLINE

LADY H

She spoils him, dear Rector, she spoils him.

MRS AL

I am sorry Sir John has gone. He has been so interesting on the subject of Ceylon. Or was it Madagascar? I think it was Madagascar.

III, 333 *It is God's Law* BLMS adds here:

I felt instinctively you would be one with me in all such things. The other women in the drawing room seemed to be sneering at me. Of course Lady Hunstanton is everything that is kind and nice and Lady Caroline is good-natured in her rough way, but I don't like Lady Stutfield and I hate Mrs Allenby.

MRS AR

They are quite happy.

MABEL

But you wouldn't accept happiness such as theirs, even if you wanted happiness.

MRS AR

What I want, oh! what I want I can never get.

III, 338 *going away with Lord Illingworth?* BLMS has an additional exchange here:

Do you like him going away with Lord Illingworth? Of course Lord Illingworth has a wonderful charm about him. But I don't like him. Somehow he makes me feel afraid. I don't think he is a good man. Do you think Lord Illingworth a good man, Mrs Arbuthnot?

MRS AR

Who is good in this world?

MABEL

None of us. But some of us try to be, and, I have no right to say it to you, of course, but I wonder, Mrs Arbuthnot, that, knowing Lord Illingworth as you do, you should give your son's life into his hands to make it or mar it. Lord Illingworth has an extraordinary influence on everyone, I am told. But do you think it is an influence for good?

C follows BLMS very closely.

III, 365–9 *But I'm ambitious . . . do everything for me* these lines are considerably longer in BLMS:

You enjoy yourself very much in the garden, and going about the parish looking after your old women, and doing all kinds of good things for other people. But I'm . . . ambitious, mother. I want something more than that. And then Lord Illingworth is so generous. Of course he knows we are not well off and he says he will only be too pleased if you would let him offer you anything you want. Why, mother, you'll be able to take the Manor House and keep a pony carriage and give blankets and coals to all the poor in the district whether they deserve it or not, which I know is what you like, mother . . . And then, you'll be able to wear pretty dresses, mother. I wish you would dress like the other women who are here. You always wear black and buy the most unbecoming things you can find, and you are much prettier than they are. I want you to wear nice things, mother, and I want you to be happy. Believe me, you'll be quite happy [*illegible*] and of course I'll write to you by every mail . . .

MRS ILLINGWORTH [sic]

Aleck, be sure of this. I will not take any money from Lord Illingworth, not a penny.

ALECK

Mother, you have taken some absurd prejudice against Lord Illingworth. Of course, when I leave the horrid Bank our income, small as it is, will be very much diminished, and it is only fair that it should be made up to you in some way. And Lord Illingworth is so nice about it all. You don't know how nice he is, and he doesn't put it as a favour.

C has shortened version of this exchange.

IV, 13–14 *I am afraid you mean something wrong* BLi and T add here lines originally used earlier in the play: 'But then I was brought up not to understand anything. I assure you, Gerald, the amount of things I and my poor dear sister were taught not to understand was quite extraordinary.' The lines are deleted in T and omitted in LC. BLii, BLMS have:

'But talking of last night, Gerald, I can't make out what happened to everyone. My pretty little American disappeared to bed without even bidding me goodnight. Lord Illingworth never went to the smoking room, James tells me. And Lady Caroline sent me a little note by her maid this morning, to say that her poodle had a severe attack of indigestion and that Sir John had been obliged to sit up with it till four in the morning . . . (*To* MRS ALLENBY).

IV, 43 *She is quite . . . isn't she?* BLii and BLMS have instead:

LADY H

How clever you are, dear! You never mean a single word you say. Really the modern education of women is wonderful. I am told nowadays that every wife knows a great deal more than her husband does.

MRS AL

A great deal more, Lady Hunstanton. Man, as a sex, has been found out.

LADY H

Ah! We found them out, too, dear. But in a different way.

In later drafts the lines were deleted. Cf. I, 146–7n.

IV, 62 *ask me to be his secretary* (I wish Lord Illingworth would ask me to go away with him. I'd start tomorrow whether I was suitable or not BLii, C, BLMS; I wish Lord Illingworth would ask me to be his secretary. I would read all his letters and never answer one of them. LADY H: Lord Illingworth's secretary? How can you suggest such a thing? MRS AL: Oh! I don't see why I shouldn't be his secretary, Lady Hunstanton. The charm about modern life is, that nowadays nothing looks so like innocence as an indiscretion. That is why one always suspects people about whom there has never been a breath of scandal. T, BLi).

IV, 79–80 *insist on your going* BLii, C and BLMS add here:

I will certainly talk to her about it when she comes down. Besides, Lord Illingworth has taken such a fancy to you. (*To* MRS ALLENBY) Hasn't he, dear?

MRS AL

Lord Illingworth would talk about nothing else but Mr Arbuthnot, the whole of yesterday afternoon. He looks on him as his most promising disciple. I believe he intends him to be an exact replica of himself, for the use of schools.

LC, T, BLi add instead, however:

I drove my eldest son to America, when he came of age, that he should learn something about human nature, and sent his brother to the colonies, that he should never know anything about it.

IV, 83 *A bad headache!* BLMS has the following additional passage:

How very interesting! I had a bad headache, myself, lately. I forget when it was. And I cured it at once with a wonderful medicine. I can't remember its name or whether it was a powder or not. But your dear mother should use it. You'll tell her to use it, won't you, Gerald? It's not to be had at any of the chemists, I know that. And you'll tell her also how sorry I am not to have seen her.

IV, 90–3 *Come, dear, I must . . . Good-bye* BLii and BLMS have instead:

Where is my sunshade. Ah, thank you. And my other glove. I wonder why it is one always loses the other glove. Oh, thank you. Yes, we mothers are culpably weak; but I'll have a long talk to *your* dear mother about it.

Moves towards door

MRS AL

Are you afraid of Lord Illingworth that you refuse such an offer, Mr Arbuthnot?

GERALD

I am not afraid of anyone, Mrs Allenby.

MRS AL

I am afraid of him. That is why I like him so much. There is a delightful sense of danger in talking to him. And danger is so rare in modern life. We all live in the most vulgar security and everyone is to be trusted.

LADY H

Come, dear, come. You mustn't flirt with Mr Arbuthnot. He is in my black books.

MRS AL

Mr Arbuthnot won't let me flirt with him, Lady Hunstanton. I wish he would. I am afraid Lord Illingworth must have told him that there is no use flirting with me. Lord Illingworth is quite wong. We women are very weak, I know, but I'm glad to say I have sufficient will-power left to yield to every temptation.

LADY H

You demoralising darling! You deserve a good scolding. Doesn't she, Gerald?

IV, 126 *force him to do it* BLii and BLMS have a further lengthy exchange here:

GERALD

I will not allow him to refuse. And then we can go away, you and I.

MRS AR

No, no.

GERALD

Yes, mother. We had no right to be here at all, with a false name, a false position, a false life. I know you never wanted to go into society and that sort of thing, mother. But still it would have been better if we had lived somewhere with poor common people. They don't mind so much, and we could have told the truth to them.

MRS AR

The poor are as hard as the rich. Harder, I often think. Suffering has made them more bitter. In this world happy people are the kindest. But don't think, Gerald, I want to stay here. I will go anywhere you wish, and live as you choose; work if it is necessary to work, starve if one of the two must starve. If there is ignominy it shall be mine. If there is disgrace, it shall be mine also. Or if you think it would be wiser for you to be by yourself, well I don't mind living alone if you will let me see you from time to time, Gerald. You needn't let people know that I'm your mother, if you don't wish it.

GERALD

Mother, there is no question of our parting. Wherever you go, I go. But before we leave here, and we must leave this place as soon as possible . . .

IV, 326–9 *For a little, then . . . to see you, ma'am* this passage underwent many revisions. BLMS has:

For a little, then: and if you let me, near you always. You are both too good to me, too good to me. Now leave me; the roses in our garden are in bloom and have no thorns. I am so tired, oh! so tired!

MABEL (*To* GERALD)

Come.

Enter ALICE *R.C.*

MRS AR

What is it, Alice?

C is very similar. In T and BLi the references to roses are omitted and the scene becomes more theatrically effective:

For a little then and if you let me, near you always. Now leave me! I am tired, oh! so tired!

HESTER (*To* MRS ARBUTHNOT)

Come out to the garden.

MRS AR

Later on, later on.

GERALD

No, now.

MRS AR

As you choose. I'll go and get my shawl. Don't wait for me.

Exeunt HESTER *and* GERALD. MRS ARBUTHNOT *goes towards door L.C. Stops at looking-glass over mantlepiece and looks into it. Enter* ALICE *R.C.*

ALICE

A gentleman to see you, ma'am.

IV, 363–4 *these democratic days* BLMS and BLii add here:

If anyone of us makes an ass of himself, or is ass enough to be found out, as poor Southwark was the other day, the moral indignation of the British public is something astounding. One would think that by going wrong, one was poaching on their private preserves. One is, I fancy. The masses, as they are termed, want to keep all the pleasant sins to themselves, and to leave us nothing but the seven deadly virtues. I assure you that as a rich commoner, Gerald will be much better off than he would be if he had a handle to his name.

IV, 435–8 *Are you serious . . . interest me enormously* BLii and BLMS have a much longer speech here:

Why? I should think you know me well enough not to expect any elaborate declaration of affection from me or any nonsense about repentance and that sort of thing. Repentance is always a confession of failure, and I never fail. I should never admit it at any rate. This is a perfectly plain business transaction, in which you have much more to gain than I have, and our son much more still. For his sake I am quite ready to marry you. After all, why shouldn't I? You are my son's mother, you are a lady by origin; I was head over ears in love with you once, and you are excessively handsome still. Hard but handsome and you would do one credit if you were better dressed. The Illingworth diamonds would set you off splendidly. You require that sort of thing. Do you know you quite amuse me by refusing. Are you serious? If so, do tell me your reasons. They would interest me enormously.

IV, 493–6 *You of all women . . . A man of no importance* the last lines of the play underwent considerable revision. The longest is in BLii:

MRS AR (*Looking up*)

Would you choose me for a mother?

MABEL

You of all women I have ever known.

MRS AR

Dear child! I owe you everything!

MABEL

You owe me nothing. My joy, my wonderful joy, has come through you. There are things so far away we cannot see their use, so near we cannot see their beauty. You have shown them to me, and knowing you, I know life's meaning better. But we will not talk of what is over. For all of us life is only just beginning . . . We will have a new life in a new land and be so happy.

MRS AR

Happiness? Is that in store for me?

MABEL

Oh! so much, mother! *Kisses her*

GERALD

Come, the sun is brighter than ever. Let us go out and bid goodbye to the old garden. You and Mabel go to London this afternoon. I will follow in three days and be near you – and oh! mother, Mabel has promised to be my wife before the roses are over.

MRS AR (*To* MABEL)

My daughter! My daughter!

They move towards the door leading into garden with their arms round each other's waist. GERALD *goes to table L.C. for his hat. On turning round he sees* LORD ILLINGWORTH'*s glove lying on the floor and picks it up*

GERALD

Hallo, mother! whose glove is this? You have had a visitor. Who was it?

MRS AR (*Turning round*)

Oh, no-one. No-one in particular. A man of no importance.

CURTAIN

C, BLi, BLMS are similar to this draft. By LC Wilde had shortened the scene considerably:

HESTER

You of all women I have ever known. My joy, my wonderful joy, has come through you. But we will not talk of what is over. For all of us life is only just beginning . . . We will have a new life in a new land and be so happy.

MRS AR

Happiness? Is that in store for me?

HESTER

Oh, so much, mother.

MRS AR

My daughter! My daughter!

GERALD

Hallo, mother, whose glove is this? You have had a visitor? Who was it?

MRS AR

A man of no importance.

CURTAIN

The corrected T typescript is very similar to LC.

APPENDIX II
WOMEN'S COSTUMES IN THE PLAY

The following extract is from an article in *The Sketch*, giving lady readers an account of the costume in *A Woman of No Importance*. It suggests the elaboration and expense of fashionable dress in the period – effects difficult to reproduce economically now, because of the amount of material involved – and the significance attached to Mrs Arbuthnot's black dress.

'Dress at the Haymarket Theatre', *The Sketch*, 26 April 1893.

> Whatever shortcomings the critics may find in Mr Oscar Wilde's play, we are prepared to maintain that it cannot by ladies be regarded as a play of no importance. It is beautifully dressed, and one has an opportunity of studying in it every variation of modern fashion. Mrs. Bernard Beere, generally so remarkable in her choice of dresses, wore two severe-looking gowns, both black. The costumes, of course, were, by stage tradition, appropriate to a betrayed woman, and had the advantage of standing out strongly in grim, sombre majesty against the brilliant dresses of the butterfly women of the play. Mrs. Tree, in the first act, as she stood on the terrace at Hunstanton Chase, seemed a dainty figure sketched by Lancret. Her dress, pure Louis XV., was of white silk chiné, with roses of every tint – a silk that reminded one of old-fashioned chintz. Her quaintly cut cloak of willow-green, open from throat to hem, with short pelerine, was edged with sable, and had a silk lining of a still softer shade; a branch of mauve orchids held in her hand gave the finishing touch of colour to the pretty picture. In the second act her dinner dress was charming in colour and design. The long train of pink satin, suspended *à la Watteau*, was bordered by trails of pink roses and lined with black satin, a combination unusual, perhaps, but perfectly successful. Its décolleté bodice of satin was finished with square revers edged by a tiny line of black jet; the revers half masked puffed sleeves of white crape, over which more roses fell in garlands.
>
> Miss Julia Neilson's first dress was delightful in colouring, for in the folds of her shot moiré all the tints of the opal seemed playing hide-and-seek. The skirt was plain and bell-shaped, and over the close-fitting bodice fell a deep frill of finely pleated crape. Her next dress, of white satin, was entirely veiled by silver-spangled tulle. In itself the dress, glistening and shimmering with every movement, was pretty, but somehow seemed hardly suited to the stately, puritanical Hester Worsley. Her last costume, 1830 in style, was of pinky yellow glacé silk. Miss Blanche Horlock's dresses were early Victorian – one of réséda satin with a berthe of thick cream guipure was especially graceful. Miss Le Thière's violet velvet gown was an ideal dress for an elderly woman.

CPSIA information can be obtained
at www.ICGtesting.com
Printed in the USA
LVHW012306071222
734769LV00004B/442

9 780713 673517